A TINY SPARK OF HOPE

A TINY SPARK OF HOPE

Healing Childhood Trauma in Adulthood

KIM S. GOLDING and ALEXIA JONES
FOREWORD BY DANIEL A. HUGHES

Jessica Kingsley Publishers
London and Philadelphia

First published in Great Britain in 2021 by Jessica Kingsley Publishers
An Hachette Company

3

A CIP catalogue record for this title is available from the British Library and the Library of Congress

ISBN 978 1 78775 431 7
eISBN 978 1 78775 432 4

Printed and bound by CPI Group (UK) Ltd, Croydon CR0 4YY

Jessica Kingsley Publishers' policy is to use papers that are natural, renewable and recyclable products and made from wood grown in sustainable forests. The logging and manufacturing processes are expected to conform to the environmental regulations of the country of origin.

Jessica Kingsley Publishers
Carmelite House
50 Victoria Embankment
London EC4Y 0DZ

www.jkp.com

Alexia:

I dedicate this book to my birth mother, in recognition of how truly different things might have been for us both should DDP have found its way into your life. I love you.

Kim:

I dedicate this book to Alexia, who has shown such courage in going on this therapy journey with me and in choosing to share her story in the hope that it will help others with their own journeys.

Contents

FOREWORD

Family relationships are so important for children. These are their first relationships and will affect the children's psychological and physical development. Children develop a bond with their parents which helps them to emotionally connect to them. These are called 'affective bonds', because the children experience them emotionally. Each bond a child forms is unique. While these are one of a kind, there are features of them which are common for all children. These features are crucial for the well-being of the child.

To develop well, children need a relationship with a parent or parents that is available from birth. These relationships provide the infants with an experience of being responded to that is contingent. This means that the parent's response is influenced by what the child is doing or signalling; if the infant cries, a contingent response is to soothe. These are reciprocal relationships, with each influencing the other: an infant cries and the parent soothes, the infant calms and the parent feeds, and so on. As you can see from this example, with very young children this is non-verbal and body based. The parent is attuned to what is going on in the infant and what is being communicated non-verbally. In the example above the parent might notice that the infant is trying to suckle on his finger whilst his crying is communicating his distress. The parent is continuously fine-tuning her own response in response to what the infant is doing. The parent is synchronised to the state and actions of the infant.

These ongoing, open and engaged interactions with a loving parent help the child to develop trust in human relationships. As the infant matures, these relationships provide the child with the experiences needed to develop his capacity to regulate his affective states. This means that when he becomes emotionally aroused, he can calm and soothe himself. A younger child needs help to do this (co-regulation), but with maturity he will gradually be able to self-regulate. Alongside this the child is learning to reflect. As his language develops, he learns to think and talk about what he is experiencing and to notice what others might be experiencing. The inner life of thoughts, feelings and wishes become understood and communicated.

You will notice that developing the ability to communicate in words is an important part of a child's early development. Children's words develop within the relationships that they are experiencing. This gives the children the ability to explore the past and think about the future. The children learn to form stories. These are stories of their life that allow the children to develop a coherent narrative about their experience. Psychologists believe that having an ability to form stories that make sense (are coherent) is good for emotional well-being.

In this book you will meet Alexia, who did not get the healthy relationship experiences that I have been describing. She experienced relational trauma. The traumatic experiences that she encountered came from within her family relationships. Relational trauma distorts, weakens or even puts a stop to the dynamic, relational, developmental process we have explored in a healthy infant and child. This trauma leads to the child developing mistrust in human relationships. The child does not have the experience needed to develop healthy capacity to regulate her affective states or to make sense of her internal experience, such as her thoughts, feelings and wishes. She also cannot make sense of other members of her family and what their internal experience might be. This makes it difficult for children to understand the meaning of the events that are occurring in their home. The stories that they develop tend to be fragmented, incomplete and embedded in feelings of shame and fear. The child does not feel good enough or deserving of love and care and is fearful of what is going to happen next. During the reading of this book you will see how some of these consequences of relational trauma had an impact on Alexia's psychological development.

In this book you will be introduced to a therapist, Kim, who helped Alexia, now an adult, using a model of therapy called dyadic developmental psychotherapy (DDP). I developed the therapy to help children who had experienced relational trauma, reducing its impact and helping the children to engage in healthy relationships. This then gives the children what they need for healthy development. It is a family model of therapy, actively involving the children's caregivers so that they are more able to meet their children's comprehensive needs. The core interventions of DDP are based on principles arising from our knowledge of the synchronised, relational processes just described in the context of the theories and research of attachment, intersubjectivity and trauma. These are theories about relationships and what happens when children are traumatised within these relationships.

However, relationship trauma does not only hurt the child during childhood. Its impact is likely to continue into adulthood. Long after the trauma stops, the child-now-adult is still likely to have difficulty with relating, regulating and reflecting. As adults, they still may have difficulty consistently engaging in the synchronised, reciprocal interactions which they lacked experience of during their early childhood. These adults still carry much fear and shame within themselves. At times, their emotions seem separate from their sense of self and erupt independently from the wishes of the self. Or their emotions remain silent and frozen when they are needed to give expression to the self. And their thoughts are too often confused and doubtful, losing the plot regarding issues that are important to the self.

This book presents how Kim engages in DDP with Alexia. Those familiar with DDP as it is used with children will see that the same characteristics of DDP used with children (PACE, intersubjectivity, co-regulation of affect, co-creation of meaning, follow-lead-follow, and developing a therapeutic conversation through affective-reflective dialogue) are also very valuable in the therapy of an adult who continues to be challenged by the traumas of childhood.

It is not surprising that Kim utilises DDP as an effective intervention with Alexia, since core relational, regulatory and reflective skills in adulthood continue to involve the same characteristics of relating that were crucial for development in childhood. The voices of both the therapist and client are presented in the following pages as they each express how both were affected by the course of the therapy. The nature of DDP is evident in their descriptions of how they were each touched by the experiential nature of the therapeutic process. The way that they both experienced the relationship with each other helped Alexia to heal from the impact of her early traumatic experience.

DDP focuses on the co-regulation of affective states associated with stressful events or trauma that may be challenging to the client. The client can think about her experience without becoming overwhelmed by the emotion of this reflection because of the regulating presence of the therapist. While these states remain regulated, DDP can then focus on co-creating new meanings of the traumatic event, whilst at the same time facilitating the client's reflective functioning. For example, a client might come to understand that they were not abused because they deserved it and therefore start to think about themselves differently. Since generally the adult's reflective skills surpass those of the child or young adolescent, the adult may well be able to utilise DDP to develop new meanings of traumatic events to a greater extent than a child. Alexia demonstrates such reflective skills as she successfully addresses the past and present challenges of her life.

Whilst developed as a family-based model of therapy, DDP has also been utilised for individual therapy for a child or adolescent when a caregiver is not present to create safety for the young person. In this book we are able to see how individual therapy for an adult may also represent an appropriate application of DDP in efforts to resolve the relational trauma that characterised the adult's childhood, no matter how many years in the past it might be.

Daniel A. Hughes, PhD

Founder of dyadic developmental psychotherapy

A Note on the Text

Alexia and Andrew Jones are pseudonyms. Their identities have been concealed and some details changed to protect the anonymity of themselves and family members.

Acknowledgments

Alexia writes

I'd like to acknowledge the people in my life who are most important to me, and who have supported me in every step of my journey in writing this book.

To my husband. Your endless love and support lights me up. You've always shown me there is a different way of existing, and for that I will always be thankful.

To my 'unconditional' best friend. For offering my own words back at me when I most need to hear them.

And to Kim. For offering me the first 'parental' relationship in which I experienced true safety, comfort and joy. And showing me that acceptance really is the Achilles heel of the mask.

Kim writes

There are always a range of people to thank when writing a book: mentors, friends, colleagues and family.

I count Dan Hughes as both mentor and friend. He has always

believed in me and supported me as I adapt his DDP model to different areas of my work. His generosity in sharing his model and allowing it to grow in the hands of others is limitless. Thanks also to Dan and to Adele Freeman for reading and commenting on our draft manuscript.

I needed support and supervision to hold me steady in my work with Alexia. I could not have done this without another friend and colleague, Jane Foulkes. Her extensive knowledge of working with sexual abuse and her steady guidance was a huge support for me.

Thanks also to the DDP community at the UK and Canada conferences for listening to our story and encouraging us that this was a book worth writing.

My family have always supported my writing. Chris, Alex and Lily always show patience with the time I give to it. Thanks also to Alex, Lily and Alexia for their amazing illustrations.

I am grateful to Steve Jones and colleagues at Jessica Kingsley Publishers for believing in another and rather different book idea and supporting us to bring this to fruition.

Above all, my main acknowledgment is to Alexia. Her trust in me is humbling. I have had the privilege to guide her through her therapy journey; I have learnt so much in the process. Her courage has been an inspiration. She is the one who has dared to share an intensely personal story, and I know this will help many others.

Introduction

THE STORY OF A THERAPEUTIC JOURNEY

It is a curiosity how two lives can intertwine, leaving imprints on each other. Alexia and Kim met several times: when Alexia was a child living in foster care; when she was engaged in work experience; as client and therapist; and now as co-authors. We shared joint interests in psychology as well as emotional experiences connected with supporting children growing up away from the birth family. The most intensive of these meetings was the three years as client and therapist. We both learnt so much during this time together. This was not just about how to heal from trauma, it was also a journey into the experience of foster care and moving into the adult world as 'care experienced'; a 'care leaver' as it is sometimes harshly called.

This is Alexia's story. A story of abuse, loss and growing up in foster care. A story about the building up of defences in order to survive. A story of moving beyond these defences in order to grow and thrive.

This is Kim's story. A story of a therapist asked to provide therapy to an adult. A story of understanding what it is like to suffer abuse and loss and to grow up in foster care. A story of learning about herself as she discovered the person in front of her.

This is a story of a therapeutic journey.

Alexia writes

Trust. I had heard this word countless times and yet when spoken without action it offered me no safety or security. When promised, I did not believe it. It had been promised and not honoured too often. It was a word to be disregarded, thrown away, shrugged off. It was a word I treated with suspicion. But an experience of someone acting in a trustworthy way, repeated time and time again? In every setting our paths had crossed, towards every person I observed her with, across many years, never seeming to falter. This was far more difficult to ignore. And as the fear of my life continuing as it was became greater than the fear of change (and my fear of knowing I would need to ask for help to do this), I could not ignore the tiny spark of hope that whispered to me that there might be someone with whom I could be vulnerable and real, and that this time they might just not let me down.

I do not remember much of my childhood, especially before I became fostered. Adults who could have helped me piece parts of the puzzle together chose not to, are now estranged, or simply cannot remember themselves. My social care records were mostly blacked out, and any information available told the story of a girl who was at first 'manipulative, pseudo adult, naughty' and later 'fine, the success story'. The professionals in my life only saw the masks I had learnt to project and missed the frightened, hurt and desperately lonely little girl underneath.

My understanding of my early life is as follows. I came into the world to a mother haunted by her own traumatic childhood and to my father who was loving but physically unavailable. Early life was characterised by emotional neglect and abuse. I parented my brothers. My father spent many hours at work and was not able to protect me. My paternal aunt was loving, warm and nurturing, but with her came an uncle who sexually abused me from when I was too young to remember.

The abuse continued until I became an adolescent, when I avoided the house and eventually told him to leave me alone. I dissociated from all memories of the abuse until I was 16. When I remembered, I sent him to prison.

My parents separated when I was five. I was asked to choose who to live with and I became ambivalent, feeling safer with my father but unable to resist pleas from my mother, who told me I would be hurting her by living elsewhere. Things became worse when my father was not living with us. We weren't allowed to see him much; rare times with him were full of warmth, joy and care.

Men came and left; a new baby sister joined our family. My mother became unable to cope; she would go 'on holiday' for unknown periods of time, and we were sent to live with multiple strangers across the country, sometimes together as siblings but often by ourselves. She was absent, then present, then absent again; in bed, leaving me to take care of the others, cold food. She was angry, cold, childlike, buying us luxurious gifts, locking me in my bedroom. It got too much and my mother ran away, leaving us behind.

I felt abandoned. I overheard her talking about her plans to leave and I blamed myself for not stopping her. I later found out she had been detained under the mental health act and was put into hospital.

We spent a short while living with my father, his new wife and her kids, but he told us he thought we'd be better off with a mum and a dad and placed us into foster care. No other family members would take care of us. Within a month he'd moved away with his new family.

I felt abandoned again. I was seven years old. I spent nine months with my brother in a cold, uncaring foster placement.

The foster carer hit my hands or isolated me if I did not do as she said. My youngest brother went to live with his paternal grandparents. We were not allowed to see him; his grandparents told the courts we were 'too bad'. Then my other two brothers and I moved to foster parents with whom I remained until I went to university. My siblings returned to our mother during this time.

I chose to remain in foster care. This was not an easy time; my foster parents were caring and full of love and gave me a different experience of how life could be, but as I became an adolescent my foster mother became conditional in her care, rejecting and ignoring me if I did not make her happy, telling me I was just like my mother. I longed to be an adult, to finally be in control, no longer powerless and at the mercy of others to do to me as they chose. Every decision became one which was focused on survival, safety, autonomy. I would make sure I would never rely on anyone again. I would be strong, fierce, unreachable, unreadable. That way I would finally be safe.

I choose to share my story with you, reader, but please know this was not a straightforward decision to make. I am a private person who does not expose herself readily. I remain unsure about sharing so publicly. I am fearful of judgement and resentful of pity. Please honour my discomfort and treat my story with care and compassion. And in return I hope that you find a story that speaks to a way of learning how not just to survive but to become alive.

Kim writes

I am a mother, daughter, wife and clinical psychologist. These aspects of myself all interconnect. Training to be a psychologist was to some extent a search to understand myself and my own family better. There are stories of relational trauma, immigration, evacuation and adoption within my family stories. Looking back, I think I was drawn towards clinical psychology to make sense of some of these stories, whether known consciously or unconsciously at the time. Maybe that is why I was drawn to work with children and families touched by relational trauma and loss. Understanding Alexia's story helped me to understand my own stories also.

A request for therapy is a daunting responsibility. As a clinical psychologist I am trained to work across the age span, providing therapeutic interventions to people from birth to old age. Post-qualification I specialised in working with children and families, with a focus on supporting parents who were raising children with different needs. I am used to and comfortable working with adults, through the lens of parenting their children. This eventually led to the development of a service supporting parents of children looked after and adopted. Within this service I had the privilege of working with many foster and adopted families. Often, I supported the parents. Sometimes I worked therapeutically with the children. When these young people grew up, some of them, including Alexia, began to seek me out. As young adults, finding their independence, they recognised the impact their early life experience was having on them and wanted help to manage this impact. This took me full circle back to my training in adult therapy.

I felt honoured when Alexia asked me to work with her therapeutically, but fearful about whether I could hold her story with sufficient care and respect. I have spent many years supporting others - parents, residential workers, teachers - to help children with experience of relational trauma. Often, they have expressed to me a fear about opening Pandora's box. A fear that what is inside the child will be uncontainable once released. I shared this same worry. Was I skilled enough to help Alexia look inside and to help her to contain the emotional experience of finding herself within the trauma we would discover?

I grew up against the backdrop of my mother's struggles with mental health and the impact upon my father of his parents' immigration into England. They both experienced World War II, and both had their own unique, and at times troubling, parenting experiences. I learnt early that emotion was best hidden and ignored, and my training as a clinical psychologist did not change this. It was only when training as a DDP* therapist that I truly confronted my attachment history and learnt to deal with my own fears of emotional expression in order to help my clients. This was a self-exploration that I would need to draw upon if I was to help Alexia revisit her own childhood and its impact upon her adult self.

For both of us this therapy journey was one of emotion and of reflection. The story that emerged and developed during the process of therapy was richer as a consequence. I am so pleased that Alexia has chosen to share this journey as I feel we will all learn and be encouraged by her story.

About this book

As we were nearing the end of therapy, we both wanted to share what we had learnt. We decided to write this book in the hope that others - therapists, clients and those supporting them - will benefit from hearing about our story.

This is a book about therapy over a three-year period. It describes the process of therapy from its beginning to its end. We explore how the therapy was led by Alexia, supported by Kim. In order to do this Kim was guided by the DDP model developed by Dan Hughes, and in which Kim is one of the leading practitioners in the UK. Although this model was originally developed to work with children who had experienced relational trauma, Kim adapted it to guide adult therapy. It also describes the way other therapeutic models were integrated within the DDP work. This includes Gestalt ideas and compassionate focused work.

---

* Dyadic developmental psychotherapy. This model is described in Chapter 1.

This book also describes the experience of therapy from the point of view of both the person offering and the person receiving the therapy. We each share our own reflections of the different stages of therapy. This is a highly personal reflection rather than an academic text. We wanted to convey what it was like to be on this journey together. Therapy was an act of discovery; each step brought new understanding and insight. Therapy was also a series of decisions; to go forward, to sit here for a while, to embrace, to reject. Kim needed to guide these decisions, including some gentle challenge, to help Alexia keep moving forward. The decisions were ultimately Alexia's to make. This book conveys something of the courage and fear of embracing new understandings and new ways of being.

Our hope is that this insight into the process and experience of one person's therapy using DDP as a guiding model will be helpful for therapists. Everybody's experience of therapy will be different, as it is always a unique experience. Going into the unknown can however be very daunting. Perhaps for those deciding to pursue therapy for themselves, this book will also help them to have some idea of what they might expect.

This is a book about early abuse and neglect and growing up in foster care. Whilst this book describes a journey in the present, we could not have made this journey without exploring the past. Within this book we do not dwell on the details of abuse and neglect; that story belongs to other people as well as Alexia. We do explore how we came to understand the impact of this abuse and neglect on the way Alexia saw herself and on her day-to-day functioning. This describes the resilience and resourcefulness of a child who had to adapt to an adverse early environment. We explore how Alexia, as a child, developed layers of defences in order to make this adaptation, and how as an adult she needed to find a way to move beyond these defences to find the person she was always meant to be. This was a search for authenticity.

Understanding is a powerful tool, guiding ways to help ourselves and to help others whom we are supporting. Adults who are trying to understand their own early experiences may find something of Alexia's story that will resonate with them. We also hope that parents who are parenting children with experience of relational trauma will find new insight here, helping them to understand their own children a little more deeply. This book may also offer insights for those supporting these children as they grow up and leave care.

The book begins with a chapter introducing the DDP model. For those familiar with the model, or who are more interested in the experience than the process of the therapy, the reader can move straight to Chapter 2. From Chapter 2 onwards, the story of the therapy is told in three ways. The chapters begin with a section of a story written by Kim over the course of the therapy. We call this story 'Finding Me'. We follow this with reflections from Alexia. Kim then gives her reflections. These chapters are interspersed with the other stories Kim wrote, the compassionate letters we both wrote and reflections from Andrew, Alexia's husband. The book can be read in sequence as it appears; if you prefer, you could follow the 'Finding Me' story, Alexia's reflections and Kim's reflections separately.

Whilst Alexia is the central character within this story, there are of course other characters who make an appearance: people who have touched Alexia's life from birth onwards. We have endeavoured to maintain the anonymity of these people throughout, but the text remains true to the key elements of her story. We want to make clear that this book is about Alexia's story: a story about the impact of childhood experience. We are not judging anyone referred to in this story, including those who were in Alexia's life as a child. We do not have enough understanding of these others and their individual stories to judge them. This is a story about the subjective experience of growing up in a birth family and then foster care. It is not about what happened or why.

It is about how what happened impacted on a child and carried echoes into adulthood. This book is an exploration of individual experience which seeks to understand Alexia, not anyone else. We anticipate that we all can move forward more hopefully when we understand ourselves more fully.

Within this book we describe how we used metaphors about 'black and white' and 'colour' to describe changes within Alexia in the way she thought about the world. It was as if a black and white world had filled with colour, much like a television programme changing from black and white into colour. We are aware that black, white and colour are also words that can be used in a way that is oppressive to black people. We would like to make clear that we are not using these words in this way. Black Lives Matter.

OUR GUIDING MODEL

Reflections from Kim

When Alexia first approached me, I wondered if I was competent to offer adult therapy. Had I enough skills, up-to-date training and knowledge to do this work justice? Alexia believed I did. I needed to believe in myself. In many ways this paralleled a lack of confidence I had when I started working with families of children in care. Then, as now, I worried that my skills were not up to the task. Then, as now, I needed a model to guide my work to be safe and effective. Then, as now, I found the same answer.

I think back to the setting up of a support service for families of children looked after and adopted. This was the same service within which I first heard about and then met Alexia, when she was still very young. To help children like Alexia and their foster or adoptive families we needed a model of work, a framework for the range of support, consultation and therapy interventions we were providing that would suit the needs of children with relational traumas and eventual separation from birth family relationships. At the same time, early in the 2000s, Dan Hughes, a clinical psychologist in the USA, was developing his model of working:

dyadic developmental psychotherapy, or DDP as it became widely known. This development stemmed from a feeling of frustration that tried and tested therapies were not helpful for children and families when the children had been exposed to relational trauma and loss of birth family.

Dan's work was a perfect match for what we were doing within the team. DDP provided us with a way of working that was relational-based, to help children with experience of relational trauma or, as it was starting to be called, developmental trauma. It provided a set of principles and a way of being that could be applied to supervision, consultation, parenting support and therapy. Over the next 20 years I trained in and applied this model of working, developing a range of resources for working with the parents of traumatised children, including those in foster care, residential care and adoption. Whilst clinical psychology training had prepared me for working as a therapist as well as a psychologist, it was only during my training in the DDP model that I learnt to confidently be a therapist. This is the confidence I needed to support Alexia in the therapy she was requesting.

DDP provided me with a way of being; a way of offering relationship that had become a part of who I was as a person, as well as a psychologist. It was therefore natural for me to use the DDP model to guide me in adult therapy.

One of the strengths of this model is that it provides a relational focus to the work whilst also allowing the integration of other models of therapy within it. DDP is the containing relational framework, whilst other models offer complementary ways of working, helping the process of integration and healing at the centre of the therapy with traumatised individuals. This integrative approach is the way that I chose to adapt DDP for the therapy with Alexia.

Within this introduction I provide a brief summary of the DDP model and principles which I refer to within my reflections. If you would like to learn more about DDP I recommend a book written by myself, Dan Hughes and Julie Hudson, *Healing Relational Trauma with Attachment-Focused Interventions: Dyadic Developmental Psychotherapy with Children and Families* (Hughes, Golding & Hudson 2019). If you already use the DDP model or if you prefer to follow the story of the therapy without focusing on the approach, you may prefer to move past the section below to the start of Chapter 2.

The DDP model

DDP is a relational therapy.

We all need relationships in order to thrive. Influencing and being open to the influence of others provides the give-and-take needed for successful relationships.

Survivors of relational trauma, like Alexia, have learned to avoid such reciprocity. As a young child Alexia withdrew from reciprocal relationships. She constructed defences that allowed her to feel in control. This gave her a fragile sense of safety to compensate for the lack of safety from within her family. This, however, came with a cost.

In order to gain safety, she stopped trusting in relationships. In this way she sacrificed reciprocity, preferring to control rather than being open to the influence of the other and, as we were to discover, she lost a sense of authenticity in the process. Authenticity comes from being true to our core values and beliefs. These guide our self-concept and influence how we relate to others. When we behave to please others, or to protect ourselves from others, we are guided by our expectation of them rather than our self-concept. We are no longer true to ourselves. Over time we identify with this inauthentic self and lose sight of who we truly are.

When Alexia sought therapy, she recognised this. She knew there was something lacking in the relationships she was a part of. She knew that to survive her childhood she had hidden parts of herself away. She felt false and empty, with a deep fear that if she was truly known others would reject and abandon her. Alexia came to therapy to seek a different relationship, one that held hope that things could be different.

Within the therapy I offered Alexia a relational experience which was unconditional. This acceptance provided a gentle challenge. I accepted without judgement how she thought and felt. This was not wrong nor right, it was just what it was. She learnt to trust in my acceptance, and in doing so met a contradiction to her own beliefs that she was so bad that no-one could ever accept her and that everyone she met would eventually find her out. Together we made sense of where these beliefs came from and how she had built defences to cope. Alexia began to revise her sense of who she was. As we came to understand these defences, Alexia's experience of trauma became integrated and transformed.

> These conversations develop a new path beyond the trauma, and on this path stories develop. DDP is about creating new stories. Traumatic events strike against our minds and hearts and create a story that is fragmented by gaps and is distorted by strong emotions from which the child shrinks and hides. These stories are rigid, with meanings given to the child by the one abusing him or her. From these jagged stories of shame and terror that arose from relational trauma, DDP is creating stories of connection, strength and resilience. As human beings, we have no choice but to create stories. Within DDP, we cocreate integrative stories...that lead to the development of an integrated sense of self and, over time, a coherent narrative. (Hughes *et al.* 2019, p.7)

Our conversations within the therapy sessions helped Alexia and me to create stories together. We explored her fragmentary memories, sensations, experiences, worries, fears and hopes;

holding these together, we discovered her stories, past, present and for the future. We were explorers using a fragmented map to discover who Alexia was. These were the stories that were co-created. I also wrote stories for Alexia, the first one at Alexia's request. These stories helped me to press a pause button and reflect on where we were. I wrote about what I had discovered in our joint work and offered this to Alexia.

The first of these was 'Finding Me', a story of all that I was learning about what Alexia had and was experiencing. I added to this at intervals during the therapy and it is reproduced here at the beginning of each chapter.

The other stories were metaphorical. The use of metaphor allowed us to view the story from a distance and gave us an opportunity to notice where we had travelled and what we had discovered together. 'The Russian Doll' and 'The Kintsugi Pot' were written within the therapy, whilst I wrote 'Beneath the Mask' for our ending. 'Armoured by Loss' was written whilst we were writing this book, as I felt that it was missing. It is the story I would have written during therapy if I had thought to.

Reflections from Alexia

A big part of why I approached Kim for support was because of her belief in the power of the DDP model. When I learned much more about childhood trauma and became interested in her work, the way of being within the DDP approach spoke to me - I recall it as a light bulb moment, a moment of realisation that there was a way of understanding and making sense of my early experiences that did not judge, criticise or shame me.

This idea shook me to my core. It did not in any way blame me for what had happened to me as a child, nor for the strategies and defences I had developed over time. Instead it offered an idea that rather than being bad or unhealthy, these defences had in fact allowed me to survive. DDP offered me a way of understanding myself, through the eyes of a healthy and safe relationship.

This sense of safety gave me the confidence to ask Kim to write me a story, never imagining she would end up writing me several! I had come across her story writing; it was beautiful and meaningful. Kim had suggested I read some of the stories in her book (Golding 2014) that might fit for me. I wanted one of my own. All the stories created for me by Kim gave me a sense of who I was. The stories proved how well Kim knew me. I knew who I was in the eyes of someone else and I found myself within the stories. They helped me to feel integrated. They fitted. I trusted Kim's acceptance and the stories confirmed this.

I hadn't had stories growing up. I don't know what my first word was. I don't know how heavy I was when I was born. How do I know who I am? How do I know that I exist? I had no sense of who I was. I had no-one who could tell me.

The stories gave me this sense of Me. Kim wrote the stories and I claimed myself in the process. I have my own stories now. The stories were so meaningful. This was so powerful. I was important enough to be in a story; not only in, I had the lead role. I can't describe how big this felt.

Summary of the DDP principles

The DDP principles were my guide to working with Alexia. Together they gave me a way of being that allowed her to feel safe enough to join me in the challenge of making sense of her past, understanding the impact of this on herself and learning to move beyond the defences that she had constructed to survive. Within my reflections I refer to these principles and how they guided me to provide Alexia with the relationship she needed at that time. Here I provide an overview of these principles for those who would like a little more explanation of these.

Intersubjective relationships: Alexia, like all human infants, was born ready for relationship. She instinctively sought to share experiences with those most closely interacting with her. She wanted and needed a reciprocal influence where each is open to the influence of the other. This is 'intersubjectivity', as described by eminent child psychologist Colwyn Trevarthen (2001). Such interactions would help her to learn about herself and the world around her.

Alexia's early environment did not provide healthy intersubjective experiences. These were either lacking or they filled her with fear, terror and confusion. Children have a deep interest in and curiosity about the world around them. Alexia grew up to become anxious and vigilant instead. She learnt to closely monitor what was happening around her for signs of threat. Eventually, she learnt to give others what they needed as this felt safer. Consequently, her own needs were hidden away. Alexia learnt to avoid intersubjective connections for fear she would be discovered as not good enough. Experiences of reciprocity threatened the fragile control she had developed that provided her with an illusion of safety.

Within therapy I needed to help Alexia feel safe enough to give up this illusion. I needed to help her to trust me so that she could experience the intersubjective relationship I offered. She would no longer have to make sense of her experience alone and through the lens of her past trauma. Instead our relationship would allow us to figure things out together. Instead of her past trauma acting as a lens, *understanding* her trauma would become our torch.

Alexia had learnt to *fear* the intersubjective, anticipating that such experiences would hurt her. Her sense of herself was built around this fear. In providing a safe, intersubjective relationship I was providing a gentle challenge to this sense of self; to the belief that all intersubjective relationships were dangerous because they would expose the badness at her core. Our relationship was the disconfirming evidence she needed to begin to revise her sense of who she was and what she might expect from others.

PACE: To help Alexia to trust me and the therapeutic process I needed an attitude, a way of being, that would help her to feel safe with me. Within DDP, this attitude is known as 'PACE'. Each letter represents a part of the whole: playfulness, acceptance, curiosity and empathy.

Curiosity represents a slowing-down within the relationship. I needed to take the time to discover what Alexia thought and felt. My *acceptance* needed to be clear, to demonstrate to Alexia that she was not going to be judged by me. With *empathy* I helped Alexia to know that I was with her, supporting her through difficult experiences. We also had moments of *playfulness*, bringing some fun and joy into the process. PACE was my guide to listen to Alexia without pressuring her to change. It allowed us to be interested in her inner life because it offered no judgement of this. PACE recognises the humanistic person-centred approach pioneered by the US psychologist Carl Rogers, including the therapeutic stance of unconditional positive regard (acceptance), congruence (genuineness) and warmth (empathy) (Rogers 1961).

As Alexia experienced her emotional world being acceptable to me, we discovered alternative stories about herself and her experience. There was no pressure to change, but this emerged naturally from our joint discovery of who she was and our imagination of who she could be. Holding to PACE was not always easy. It required me to be *open and engaged* to whatever Alexia brought to me. Alexia would hold views about parts of herself that were difficult to hear. I did not need to agree with these. I did need to accept without judgement that these were her beliefs. To try and talk her out of this would be a defensive response, threatening my open and engaged PACE attitude. I would be responding to reduce my anxiety rather than to help Alexia feel understood and validated. I needed to notice when I drifted towards defensiveness, so that I could return to being open and engaged.

As Alexia experienced my attitude of PACE, she became open to the intersubjective experiences that I was offering. This in turn provided increased *safety*. When Alexia was fearful within our sessions, she would either become more hyper-vigilant and aroused, reacting to her emotional state, or shut down and dissociative, as she cut off from her emotions. These are closed, defensive states. At these times I needed to stay with her, allowing our relationship to provide the *co-regulation* of her emotional experience that she needed. My regulated state would help Alexia to calm her own emotional arousal. She would feel safe with me and this allowed her to move back into emotional balance. She became calm and open to reflection once more.

This relationship experience provided opportunities for the *co-creation* of Alexia's narrative. This relied on the process of mentalisation, as we explored Alexia's inner world of thoughts, beliefs, feelings and fears. Mentalisation is described by Peter Fonagy and others in mentalisation-based interventions (Bateman & Fonagy 2011). With this approach I could help Alexia to be curious about her internal experience and the stories she had developed to make sense of her life. We could wonder together about alternative stories to account for what has and is happening. In this way we co-created a new story to understand both her past events and current experience. Alexia never experienced any pressure to abandon one story in favour of the other. This process allowed her to become aware of alternative stories to make sense of her experience. She developed more flexibility, and new possibilities opened up to her. In this aspect of DDP I am very much reminded of narrative therapy, with its emphasis on therapist and client co-authoring new narratives that the client holds for herself, as devised by the late Australian social worker and family therapist Mike White (2004).

To provide sufficient safety so that we could join together in co-regulation and co-creation, I was helped by:

Using a story-telling voice

This lyrical tone and rhythmical way of talking held Alexia's attention and helped her to experience my genuine interest in understanding her.

Creating affective-reflective (A-R) dialogue

I needed to attend to the content of what Alexia was sharing with me whilst also attending to her emotional experience, conveyed verbally and non-verbally. This affective-reflective (A-R) stance allowed Alexia to experience the affect associated with the emotional parts of her story whilst reflecting on the content of her story. This helped her to integrate and process this experience so that it became less troubling to her. A-R dialogue helps in the co-creating of the narrative. In this it has clear echoes of Diane Fosha's accelerated experiential dynamic psychotherapy model. In both of these approaches, the client is helped to develop coherent autobiographical narratives by integrating affect and cognition (Fosha 2000).

Adopting a follow–lead–follow approach

Alexia was not helped if I told her what to think or feel. This directive approach felt very invalidating. She found it difficult, however, to know this for herself. She had so little experience of a parent helping her to make sense of her experience when she was young that this was not something that came to her easily. Alexia would struggle to use a non-directive approach. She needed help to discover the meaning of her inner world. I needed to be both non-directive and directive. I would start where Alexia was, listening to her communications. I would accept the fledgling narrative she offered to me (*follow*). This helped Alexia to feel understood. I would then wonder about this narrative, *leading* her into a deeper understanding which was both affective (empathy) and reflective (curiosity). As Alexia responded to this I would then *follow* again.

Talking with, about and for

Alexia needed me to gently lead her into her emotional experience, helping her to tolerate this without becoming overwhelmed. In order to do this, I needed to be aware of Alexia's window of tolerance: the amount of emotional experience she could manage in that moment. I needed to notice when she started to move beyond this window. At these times it helped if I stopped talking directly to her. I could 'talk about' her by wondering out loud or, if Andrew, Alexia's husband, was present, talking to him whilst Alexia listened. In this way Alexia witnessed her story being understood. This 'talking about' reduced the emotional intensity and was less overwhelming for her. At times I judged that Alexia could move deeper into her window of tolerance. 'Talking for' can facilitate this. I would give Alexia a voice by talking for her, allowing her to have words for her experience when she couldn't find these for herself. This was an emotionally more intense experience, co-regulated by me. By moving between talking with, about and for, I could help Alexia experience her story affectively and reflectively, without becoming overwhelmed emotionally.

Attending to verbal and non-verbal communications

I would listen attentively to what Alexia was communicating. This communication was both verbal and non-verbal. There were times when I would notice discrepancies between these. At these times it was helpful to notice and reflect on this. Attending to both verbal and non-verbal communications deepened our understanding.

Providing relationship repair

Relationship ruptures are a normal part of human interactions. Misattunement, when emotional connection is lost, occurs because of a misunderstanding or because one or both has become defensive. Inevitably there were moments of rupture in my relationship with Alexia. It was my responsibility to notice these and to repair them. By acknowledging the difficulty that had arisen I was communicating to Alexia that I was committed to the relationship. The repair focused on bringing our relationship back into attunement again.

Together, these principles gave both of us a guiding model which strengthened our relationship, increased safety and ultimately allowed Alexia to face her worst demons, transforming her sense of who she was, had been and could be in the future.

Chapter 2

THE BEGINNING

FINDING ME

My development begins before I am born. I come into the world whole. I am. But I am not allowed to be. I have to develop parts of myself to survive. I lose Me in the process. I want to find Me again. I find someone. She is kind, but will she like the Me we find together? I ask for a meeting, just an academic discussion outside of any therapeutic relationship to help me with some work issues. This is all I can cope with just now. We soon discover that it is therapy I need.

Reflections from Alexia

I moved into adulthood with so much ahead of me. I had survived my childhood and I looked ahead, to a career, marriage, independence. Yet I felt at breaking point; overwhelmed. I felt as if I was going to crumble if I didn't do something different. I noticed that my reactions to things were different to other people. I felt odd. It's hard to explain. Things that seemed small to other people rocked my universe. It was hard to cope with the everyday. A passing comment, meant in good humour, about something I hadn't done perfectly - I found it intolerable to deal with. I would go over and over it in my head. I felt so unsettled by what they had said. It was hard to face that person again. If possible, I wouldn't see them again.

Generally, the more out of control I felt, the more in control I had to be. My home was my safe place. I had control over it: where things were placed, the way it was cleaned. I struggled to cope with visitors invading this. It disrupted the control I had. A cushion would be moved, a cup placed down wrongly. I only let a handful of people in. Self-reliance was another way of being in control. I couldn't let anyone do anything for me, whether practical or emotional. Something simple like picking up my car from the garage - I had to do it.

The control helped me to keep emotion away. I lived in my head. I thought and thought but felt little. I had little connection to my body. But then, despite my efforts, emotion would become overwhelming. It burst and I was out of control. Anxiety flooded me. I would sob uncontrollably, until I was exhausted. All of this by myself. Even with Andrew, I would turn away from him. He could not help. I knew my truth, that I was to blame for everything.

The only time I felt close to feeling content was when I was by myself, and yet this was also when I felt the loneliest. I wouldn't admit it, but I felt incredibly unhappy. Actually, I don't know if it was unhappiness, I just felt completely alone. I knew this wasn't okay. I didn't want to be like this. I wanted help. I wanted to understand why I was feeling this way. I wanted to know why I was different from others.

I remember just knowing that if anyone can help it would be Kim. Living in foster care, Kim had from time to time been there, in the background. I remember meeting her as a child. I told her that I played tennis. She was interested. Later, in my professional life, our paths crossed again. If I trusted anyone to help me it was Kim.

I was attracted to her openness, humbleness and willingness to be real. On one occasion I heard Kim talking about her attachment history. I thought she's not perfect either, and that was huge. She talked about the quiet children; the ones who seemed to be doing well. How easy it was to overlook them. This really struck me. It felt as if she was describing me. I felt that Kim would not overlook me. She would get me. This was scary too. If anyone was going to discover me, it was her. I wanted this and I feared it.

When the fear of things staying the same became greater than the fear of being vulnerable, I asked for help.

The thought of asking for therapy and being told no was intolerable and so I asked if we could collaborate professionally; it felt more acceptable. If Kim said no it would just be professional, not about me. And I was having real difficulties with the emotional issues of some of those I was working with. I found them massively triggering. This was to the point that I didn't want to see them. I wanted to do better. I thought if Kim could help me to get rid of the difficulties that I was experiencing I would be more perfect. No-one would doubt me. This was the only way I knew how to succeed. I sought help to perfect the mask I showed to everyone. I thought Kim could help me do this. How wrong I was. The journey I was setting out on was so different to what I expected.

The first session, I was so anxious. I remember ringing the doorbell and stepping two feet back, hiding a little bit. My biggest fear was that it was the wrong time, or the wrong day, and I would be sent away. I worried about every word I was saying. I worried about Kim looking at me. I worried about staying too long. I worried that Kim would think I was making a mountain out of a molehill; other people had worse problems. Paradoxically, I also worried that I would be too much for her. This was the confusion I was in; I could worry about being too much whilst also worrying that I was making a big deal out of nothing. These are the messages I got from other people: there is nothing to worry about, darling, zip it up and crack on. Underneath there was another message: don't show us, it will be too much.

Looking back, I can see I was a mass of confusion and fear. I had learnt to be compliant, and in the process my needs had been totally missed. I was busy working out what everyone needed from me whilst inside I was utterly disorganised. The more people I had to please, the more disorganised I became. No-one saw the disorganisation. They saw charming, delightful, intelligent. Even enough cheekiness so that they didn't worry about me. I brought this to my sessions with Kim. I worked incredibly hard to get my words to make sense, to sound competent. I wanted to keep Kim happy; a model client. I felt clumsy, awkward. I didn't know how to come in. I didn't know how to leave; I didn't know how this worked. I had to figure this out. Kim told me we would figure it out together. This threw me. She wasn't just going to tell me! She respected my thoughts and ideas. She saw me as her equal!

Following this session there was never a choice about coming back. I needed this even though it frightened me. Attending these early sessions felt harder than the first time. We had started to build a relationship and so I had much more to lose. In coming back, I was investing in the relationship, in something real. Now Kim knew what I was asking for, the risk was even greater that she would turn me away. Rejection would have been more painful. Trust was going to take time to grow. I had trusted her from a distance, now I had to trust her close up.

Reflections from Kim

A serene swan, paddling furiously beneath the water, is a well-used image. It is, however, a perfect image for how Alexia felt when she had her first session with me. I of course only saw the serene swan. Alexia arrived composed and calm. She was clear about what she wanted from the meeting and very reflective about the impact some of her professional relationships were having on her.

I only had glimpses of the anxiety underneath this calm exterior. I did not see how much her worried mind was working. I did not know that her careful thinking was accompanied by a frantic reviewing of everything she was going to say to ensure it would be okay. I was unaware that, for Alexia, there was genuine fear that this first meeting would be the last; that I might find a reason not to invite her back. She only told me about these worries later.

Her strengths were there, at this beginning, also: the courage to get in touch, to turn up and, even in this first meeting, to reveal some of the vulnerability that sat underneath her request to work with me; the assertiveness that helped her to function successfully in the world, laced though it was with anxiety; the compassion which motivated her work. She could not yet turn this compassion onto herself, but it was there to be nurtured and strengthened.

In her email to me, Alexia had requested help with her professional role, help which was genuinely required. She was working in a role which was not properly supervised and where she was expected to do things above her level of training and competence; sadly, not an unfamiliar situation for many people. This request therefore expressed a need, but even at this first session it was clear that a hidden need to move into therapy was also present.

Alexia had a motivation to find out who she was, why she was different from other people, and, yes, a wish to be helped to perfect the defences she had been using all her life. Whilst I could not help her with this latter aim, I trusted that within this request for help there was a seed of knowing that she needed to find a different way of being. I would help her to find this seed and together we would help it to grow. Together we would find the hidden needs that lay beneath the expressed needs that she brought to this first session.

Our first couple of sessions were divided between work mentoring and therapy. Within the former I offered Alexia a time to reflect on her work. She spoke fluently about the current stress she was experiencing. Already I could see a tendency to be hard on herself. She was quick to assume that she was at fault, and worried that she would let others down. I also saw the courage that would carry her through the next three years with me. She looked fragile but there was strength at her centre. She could be assertive, able to take risks, and had a strong commitment to her work. This all came at a cost, however. Anxiety would eat her up: had she done the right thing, would others still like her, would she be 'found out'? She already had the strengths. I needed to help her to reduce the costs of using these.

As we explored the work she was doing, we began to reflect on its impact. We started to explore who she was and the influence of her early experience. We noticed the anxieties and fears that work brought up for her, verging on panic attacks at times. Alexia recognised that she struggled with conflict, especially when there was a high level of expressed emotion. We made sense of these anxieties in the context of her childhood experience.

I tried to keep this reflective without going too deeply into the emotional content. I was conscious of my role. I wanted to think with Alexia but was wary of encouraging her to feel this too deeply. I was not successful: Alexia was ready, not only to feel her story, but to share what she felt with me. The line between work mentoring and therapy was feeling blurred. I suggested we slow down and think together about what she wanted from her sessions with me. Alexia made the decision that she was seeking therapy. We were ready to begin.

In many ways, despite her mature exterior, Alexia came to me like an infant. As a newborn, she had an instinctive trust that I could help her, not yet grounded in experience of me. Infants will quickly adapt when this trust is not reciprocated. They defend instinctively against the hurt and pain of being let down, of their needs not being met, of not feeling loved and attended to. This had been Alexia's infancy, and she brought her defences, along with her trust, to this new relationship with me. I needed to respond to Alexia's tentative trust helpfully, being careful not to give her need to reinforce the defences. I needed to help her to believe in her own lovability; that she was deserving of my attention. Just as a mother with an infant, I needed to recognise the needs that Alexia came to me with. Unlike an infant, these needs were distorted by a lifetime of adaptation and defence. We needed to look beneath these to find and integrate the fragmented and lost parts of herself.

I had briefly come across Alexia and her siblings when they lived together in foster care. I had been involved tangentially with the network around her placement. I had heard about this good child, who appeared to be doing well in foster care. She was bright and sporty. She was not the one who was concerning people. I had worried about her. I had recognised how easy it was for her to disappear behind the challenges presented by her siblings. As van der Kolk says, 'The acting out kids tend to get attention; the blanked out ones do not bother anybody and are left to lose their future bit by bit' (van der Kolk 2014, p.73). I had not heard examples of Alexia seeking help from her foster carers. It had seemed to me that she may well have 'blanked out'.

I had helped the network to consider her as a child with an avoidant attachment pattern of relating: a child who was self-reliant and compliant, who needed help to trust in dependency and to learn to turn to others for nurture and support (see Howe 2005). Now she sat in front of me as an adult and I heard about this same pattern; she sought to be perfect, making few demands on anyone, hoping she would be good enough to be acceptable to others, trying to ward off the abandonment she feared. Self-reliance and compliance were her companions still. On this first session I wrote in my notes:

This led us into an exploration of Alexia's attachment history and her avoidant presentation. We thought about the strengths of this but also the vulnerability. Alexia is aware that she is uncomfortable with emotional expression and reluctant to seek help from others. She understands that this links to her need for control, even over small things in her life. We explored her feelings of not being good enough, and the small child within her who had to be strong enough to take care of herself, but who has never been taken care of. Alexia reflected that she was tired of always being the grown-up and of missing her childhood.

Alexia was able to reflect as the adult she was; beneath lay many childhood needs that had been unmet. Understanding these would be a beginning step towards finally allowing them to be met.

Alexia also brought along to our sessions the courage, tenacity and strength that had helped her to maintain these defences so rigidly throughout her childhood. The difference was, although she did not yet realise it, she was now ready to apply these same qualities to finding out what life could be like without the defences. She was taking her first steps into a brave, new world.

I was nervous beginning therapy with Alexia. I embraced the opportunity. I wanted to help this brave young woman who had sought me out. I also knew I would be outside of my usual comfort zone. In my own way, I too was the serene swan who was staying afloat only through the hidden paddling beneath the water. I would be drawing on distant training in adult therapy, supported by more recent reading, studying and the occasional workshop. I needed a model to work within to give structure to this therapy. I looked to dyadic developmental psychotherapy (DDP) to provide this.

As a certified DDP therapist, DDP was an obvious choice. I was aware that there would be differences in using this model with an adult outside of the child and family work I was more familiar with. Not least, there would be the absence of a parent as attachment figure to support the work. There were, however, many similarities between DDP and other models of adult therapy. The work of Carl Rogers had been an influence on its development, and I was confident that this provided some validity for its adaptation to adult therapy (Rogers 1961).

The DDP principles would guide me in developing an unconditional therapeutic relationship with Alexia that would offer attachment security and intersubjective connections. This would be our secure base, allowing us to explore together all that Alexia was, is and could be.

Alexia sought therapy because of a need to discover herself, to find authenticity. She felt fake and wanted this to change. She was at a turning point in her life. A care-experienced adult, she was learning to be independent, forging a home and career. She was also planning to marry. She had entered adult life, although in many ways she still felt like a child. She wanted to understand her childhood experience. She wanted to understand why things other people found easy were hard for her. She needed to make sense of a self that did not feel real in many ways.

Alexia already knew that explanations for this lay in her past. She wanted to understand more fully what had happened to her. To this end she had already requested to read her social care notes. We thought this might be a good starting point for our work; an opportunity to understand her story at a cognitive level, before diving into its emotional depths. I hoped her notes might give us a structure for this.

In the event, it was to be many months before she finally got her social care notes, partly because of the inefficiency of the system, and partly because of Alexia's ambivalence. She wanted to read them, to fill in some gaps in her knowledge and understanding. But she also feared what she might find between the lines; she dreaded confirmation that everything was her fault. She delayed chasing the notes when they were slow to appear.

Alexia did not bring this same ambivalence to her sessions,

perhaps because of the containment provided by our relationship. She was no longer doing this alone. Alexia always turned up on time and never missed a session. Despite my plan to begin reflectively and to move into the emotional experience more slowly, I found myself following her into deeper emotional waters. I thought we needed time to learn to swim, but she was ready to dive. This came at some cost; memories and dreams would accompany Alexia between sessions as the emotional work continued. I knew I was helping Alexia to develop trust in me. I learnt I also needed to trust her. I had to trust that she had the strength to do this and that she would guide me to what she needed. I had to listen to her and to follow where she led me. I had to trust the therapeutic process that had begun.

In our first few months together, we spent much of the sessions exploring Alexia's memories. Alexia would sit quietly in the chair opposite me, lost in thought, as she reflected on her childhood. There was no order to this. She would talk about what came to mind, in that moment. I would listen, sometimes pausing her to ask a question or make a reflection. I held the pieces of her past as she gave them to me. As we sorted through these, her story emerged. Within this story the many ways of being that Alexia had used to help her cope within three different families were also remembered. A complex picture was emerging of a child who had learnt to cope against the odds.

This was a relatively gentle beginning, piecing together the story of a childhood which began in her birth family, moved through a harsh short-term foster placement and ended up in a long-term foster placement. Emotion was present – sorrow, anger and pain – but this was not the turbulent emotion that she would experience later.

Alongside her reflections of the past, Alexia was also trying to figure out her current relationships, with her fiancé and past foster carers. Alexia welcomed the sessions with me as a time of calm, where I would help her to make sense of this current experience.

Often our making sense of this would also involve reflecting about the impact of her childhood experience. The present was illuminated by the past.

As Alexia's trust in me developed, she began to see me as an attachment figure whom she could rely on. This was new for her. Relying on mothers had not been part of her childhood experience. An infant part of herself longed to have me all to herself. She felt jealous of other clients I might be working with. She worried that she would be forgotten when not with me. She found it hard to tell me this, worrying that I would be displeased with her. She did not yet trust in my non-judgement. As an adult, Alexia recognised and discussed her longing for a mother, whilst recognising that I could not fulfil this role. Alongside this, younger parts of Alexia were asking more from me as unmet needs emerged. Together we held the sorrow of this.

We were four months into therapy when we had our first test. I was going away for several weeks and we would be taking a break in our sessions. Alexia recognised that she did not want to come to the final session before this break as she felt I was abandoning her. We easily made sense of this given her childhood experience of loss and separation. Endings, even temporary ones, were hard for her.

I suspect Alexia was feeling angry towards me for leaving. She did not confide this; she could talk about feeling annoyed, but it was hard for her to admit to angry feelings. Anger, whether her own or that of others, felt very dangerous. If she felt anger with me, and even more if she displayed anger, she believed I would reject her. These fears of abandonment meant that anger was suppressed, not noticed by Alexia. She described not knowing how she felt. She was also aware that on occasions anger would burst out, apparently randomly. For example, she would get angry with Andrew over something minor. Feelings related to a different situation emerged in the relative safety of her relationship with Andrew.

To help her to manage the separation from me, I planned with Alexia that I would choose a small gift to bring back for her. In this way she would know that I was thinking of her whilst I was away. I asked her to choose her favourite animal to help guide me in my choice of a gift. As she chose a bear, Alexia told me that she felt like she was five years old. We noticed that this was the age at which she had been asked to choose which of her parents to live with. I was meeting parts of Alexia which had helped her to survive a childhood of abuse and neglect. Exploring these parts would be the second phase of our work together.

Chapter 3

DISCOVERING THE RUSSIAN DOLL

FINDING ME

The Russian Doll emerges from inside out. In therapy I discover the Russian Doll from outside in.

Baby Doll: I am born, ready for a stressful life. Nine months bathed in my mother's cortisol has begun to prepare me for what is to come. But nothing can prepare me for this.

Small, vulnerable, weak, I reach out to be taken care of. I meet confusion, contradictions. Mother is good and kind; I reach out for her. Mother is remote, and unavailable; I seek her. She is not there. Mother is cruel and punishing; I try to avoid her.

I am so little; I can't do this by myself. I can't meet my mother's need of me. I want her to see how much I need her. I am lost, alone. What can I do to make Mother appear? What can I do to make her go away? I hate my vulnerability, my powerlessness. I am unlovable. I am undeserving of love and care. I need to go away. Bury this weak, needy self where no-one can see it.

I am growing, I am getting stronger. I won't be weak and vulnerable any more. I won't need any more. But I am so little, the baby part won't go away. I try to be strong. Why can't I be stronger? I need Mother. I won't need Mother. She is here. She is kind. She finds presents for me, perfect presents, and then is angry if I am not grateful.

Mother is a beautiful painted doll, living in a beautiful painted house. I go to her, try to enter, but there is nothing inside. Where is she?

Is Mother the tiger I see in my dreams? The tiger is beautiful, strong, protective. The tiger is fierce and punishing. I love her. I fear her. Am I hers, to protect, or prey to be killed? I cannot trust her.

Who is Mother?

I have a brother now. Mother and Brother are close. She is good, I am bad. No, Mother is here with me. She whispers in my ear. I am special. I mustn't tell Brother. But now she is with her. I am so confused. What do I have to do to be special? I want my brother gone. I want to protect her. I am a good parent. I am a bad little girl. What do I have to do?

Change, change, change. You are here. You are gone. Where are you? Who are you? Who can I turn to? Father is here, but he is away. He is kind but he is remote. Sometimes it is frightening. Arguments. Silence. Alone. Strangers. I don't know what to do. I ask question after question, but I get no answers. I am alert, watching, noticing. It all changes again. Who can I rely on?

I seek others, strong, protective, kind. But he hurts me. This can't be right. I am all alone. No-one helps me. I have no-one. It hurts, it hurts. Why am I so bad? Auntie, can I rely on you? You offer me something no-one else does. You cannot protect me.

I will not feel it. I will not be weak and vulnerable any more.

I will be strong. Do what you like to me, I will not be a part of it. I will not be there. You cannot hurt me. I do not feel. I will not rely on anyone. I will not be little any more.

Angry Doll: I am angry. I am strong. I am in control. No more weakness. I will get what I need. You will take care of me.

I go to school. You will be my friend. Fine, don't be, I will find someone else. Teacher, you ask me a question. I am not sure. I will not answer. In the playground I fall. You are all laughing. Run away. Hide. Stay in charge.

Notice me, notice me. You will notice me. They do not see the little girl. She has gone. I am bigger now. They see anger, jealousy. They will give me what I need. I am naughty. Good, it makes me strong. I can hide, you won't find me. I am in control. You will not forget me. I am powerful.

Mother is sleeping again. I can't concentrate. I am worried. I need to look after the others. I can't. I am too little. Stay angry, stay angry, stay angry. Mother and Father are separating. I must choose. Don't make me choose. I am only little. I need you both. Okay then, I will look after Mother. I am not little. I am grown up. I am not five, I am twenty-five. I am strong. I can do this.

I move to foster care. A glimmer of hope. Will you take care of me? No, you see how bad I am. You are cruel, you punish. I am selfish. I am manipulative. I am unreliable. These are bad things. No-one will ever want to take care of me.

Learn not to trust. Stay angry. I must stay in charge. I must be right. I must take care of myself.

I am so sad. I want to live in a village with no sadness. Where is the village? Why can't I be there? I can't be sad. Sad is weak. Stay angry, stay angry, stay angry. Don't need, don't grieve, don't be sad. Anger, anger, anger.

We move again. I do not expect. I do not trust. I am sick, I hide. Notice me; don't notice me. I am so confused.

Anger is letting me down. I am strong. I am powerful. I am overwhelmed. I can't handle these big feelings.

Brother, leave me alone, I hate you. Blackness comes, I hurt. I don't want to hurt you. I don't want to kill you. I need to take care of you and our other brother. I don't want to be angry any more, but I don't want to feel sad, to need. Anger made these feelings go away. How can I give up anger?

I need to find another way. I will find another way of being in charge. I do not trust. I will take care of myself. I will disappear.

Golden Doll: I am self-reliant. I learn to please. I make myself helpful. I will fix things. I will care for all of you. You help me, foster carer, to develop this part of myself. It pleases you. You think it is me. You take care of Empty Doll in the empty house. Where am I?

I wear my goodness like a mask. I am not the mask, don't you see? You only see the mask. It is safer that way. I hide my sadness. I hide my anger. Deep inside I want you to find me, but I am so frightened. If you find me, you will discover how bad I really am. I will be good, I will please, then you will like me, only it isn't me, not really.

I am so tired. Pleasing others is exhausting. I strive to get it right. I strive to please all of you. How can I please all of you? If I please you I won't please another – how can I be everything to everyone? I need to be on my own. I am in my room. I hide. I read. You are out there still needing me. I will come soon. Let me be alone, then I will come.

Another choice, please don't ask me to choose again. My brothers are going home to Mother. I fear for them. Should I follow? Will they need me? I don't want to move again. I want to stay here. I have learnt to be safe here. I choose to stay. Mother is angry. Please don't ask this of me. I am allowed to stay.

Empty Doll: Everyone is pleased by the golden child, but they don't see me. They think I am happy. They don't notice me. They don't worry about me. I have zipped everything up completely. I am so scared that if you see me you will get rid of me too. I don't want to live anywhere else. I am so tired of moving. I long for someone to see the sadness, the pain. This is frightening. How will you like me if you see this? I tighten the mask.

I am numb. I walk the path but notice nothing. I don't know where I am going. I don't remember where I have come from. I concentrate on staying safe, surviving until there is nothing else. My feelings are long gone, deep inside of me, out of sight. I hope that they have gone for good, but they betray me. They sneak up on me, leaking out so that my body feels them. I have headaches, stomach ache, I am sick. I am so tired. Why don't you go away for good?

Painted Doll: And so, all is hidden as best I can do. I am false, but where is the heart of me?

Mother showed me a way. I will live in a painted doll's house with nothing inside. This is me now. I am lost. Have I become Painted Doll?

Have I become like my mother? This frightens me. I am bad. I am manipulative. I deceive. I daren't reveal the truth for fear I will lose all. And yet, there are contradictions. Is it badness, or am I vulnerable and needy? Am I manipulative; or does my control help me to survive? Do I deceive or am I just frightened of what others might see? I seek either/or but can I live with both?

There are some who see the contradictions and love me anyway. I find my father again, a man of contradictions himself. I discover a renewed relationship with him. I have friends, people with whom I can relax, although social situations tire me. I cannot truly be myself.

And then one comes, and the mask slips. I am amazed. You see the sadness. You hold me in mind. I am shocked and frightened. I push you away. You stay anyway. I let you into my life. Others disapprove. He reaches out and cares for me. He has seen the best and the worst of me.

Dare I marry you? You give me hope. You help me to search for what I need. To find my authentic self.

Reflections from Alexia

Thinking back, I find it hard to remember the first few months of therapy. In a way it is exactly like I remember my childhood, blurry, hazy, vague, dreamlike. Like wading through fog.

I had to work really hard to remember anything specific. When I talked about my childhood, there were random memories, but they weren't grounded in meaning. They just floated. I talked about them as they came to me. Then they would float away again. It's like having mail without a sorting office. Post needs to be delivered all over the world, but there is no method of sorting it to get it there. I had no mail or an overload of mail. Either I couldn't remember or the memories just came flooding back.

In the therapy room I found calm in this chaos. We were starting to build the sorting office. This was the start. I started with memories but found it hard to form these into a narrative. Together we began to work out the narrative.

I remember feeling paralysed when Kim told me she was going away. She gave me plenty of warning, but I just felt dread as it approached. In my head I knew that this was a reasonable thing for her to do, but in my heart, I felt sure that she would not be coming back. I couldn't handle it when Kim suggested getting me a small gift. I couldn't believe she wanted to do this for me. It felt intolerable. I didn't deserve Kim to come back, never mind her bringing me a gift. I felt really young, like a child. I felt so needy. I felt quite powerless in that moment, as I was taken back to my childhood.

Kim's offer of a gift was a promise that she would return. I couldn't make it happen. I had experienced so many false promises. As a child you can't make adults keep their promises, you can only blindly follow them. Too many adults had promised to come back and they hadn't. Looking back, I can see how huge this was, especially as my foster parents had left us in respite to attend a family event just a few months into placement. I remember how anxious I was whilst they were away. I had a weekend of worrying that they might not come back.

When Kim told me that she was going away I just switched off. I had to stop myself from caring; act like it didn't matter. I couldn't feel it. I was back in my head again. I knew she would come back; it was her job, she had to. But emotionally I was terrified that she wouldn't.

Did I feel angry with Kim for leaving? Honestly, I don't know. If there was something that would push Kim away, I believed it would be anger: if I showed her anger or made her angry. From infancy I had experienced anger linked with not being wanted. I think this led to me not just hiding anger, but not recognising that this was what I was feeling.

When Kim came back, I just couldn't believe it. Kim was holding up a mirror, but I was seeing something different. It showed me I was good enough to come back to. I hadn't pushed her away. Kim had not let me down, and I found this so hard. The gift became the metaphor for not being let down. I couldn't look at it for fear I would find a fault with it. It was overwhelming and I felt so young.

She had brought me an actual present. It felt huge. I felt like a child who was being looked after and delighted in. Looking back, it was the loveliest experience. It was overwhelming because I hadn't had these experiences before. It felt really nice, but I didn't know how to manage it. I don't feel like I had ever had a break and a repair genuinely before. It was so important to have this experience and it was so challenging to how I saw myself.

I felt a bit clumsy as we got back into the therapy again. It was hard to know how to go back to where we had left off. Old anxieties had resurfaced. Re-experiencing the lack of judgement from Kim gently eased me back. It was the acceptance, the lack of conditional. There were no demands made of me as safety increased once more.

At the start of each session I would feel two steps back from the end of the session before. It always took me time to settle in. Together we started to notice that talking about the present helped me to settle into the session. I needed this; the time between each session felt like a mini separation. I needed time to feel safe again. Talking about the present, catching Kim up with what was happening in my life, was important to give me this space. I was learning how to connect, and this felt lovely.

A part of me did not want to move on to more difficult territory. It felt like risking this connection. I would delay us going into the emotionally deeper part of the session. It was hard enough to feel comfortable with Kim, but even harder to feel vulnerable with her. I needed Kim to guide me. I wouldn't have taken the risk by myself. Kim's leading was also the permission I needed to know that I could open up emotionally.

Then it would pour out, like a flood. I remember crying, even before I consciously experienced the emotion. It almost happened despite myself. I remember how surprised I felt when the tears kept coming. They didn't stop. Once I had let this out, I would feel calm and grounded. At first Kim noticed this for me. I didn't recognise calmness. It wasn't something I was used to experiencing. I just felt present.

Then it was time to leave. I didn't want to leave the calmness and safety I had found. I didn't want to face the world again. I wasn't sure how to navigate leaving; each leaving felt like another rejection. More than this, I felt I owed Kim something before leaving. Unconditional felt new. I was used to having to pay for getting what I needed. If I left, I feared I wouldn't be allowed back. Ending the sessions was full of anxieties. I wanted to hold on to it and never let go. Kim had to help me to leave. She would let me know it was time to finish without me feeling judged, rejected or not good enough. Knowing we had our next sessions booked in also helped me to leave with the security that I would be back. I couldn't look at Kim; the fear of what I might see was still there. I still couldn't completely trust that I was acceptable to her.

Sometimes Kim would share something of her own experience; things that resonated with my own story. This drew me in, as I felt she might understand me. People with 'perfect' relationships felt like a threat to me. Knowing that Kim had her own flaws made me feel that mine might be acceptable to her. It felt really powerful when she shared even a little of her own experiences. It always felt as if it was in my best interest, not hers. I was alert to needs in other people, always looking for an opportunity to take care of them. Kim never gave me this opportunity. She was explicit when sharing her experiences that this was to illuminate my own. It was always about me. I felt I could trust Kim because of this sharing. Even more, I knew Kim got it.

We settled into a pattern, connecting and then exploring my experiences, present and past. I shared memories and we explored meanings. Gradually a picture emerged which we could explore more deeply. I was ready to be introduced to the Russian Doll.

I think back to Kim's Russian Doll. I hated it when I first saw it. I didn't want to believe that there was anything inside. Maybe I could accept the idea of the golden child and the angry child, but I could not consider the idea of the baby. I didn't believe that there was a vulnerable part of me; didn't believe or didn't want to believe. I'm not sure. The idea of the whole Russian Doll, it seemed to make sense but at the same time it didn't feel real. On the one hand, was this just Kim being really nice and giving me an excuse, a reason for me to feel better? Could it really be that I was not to blame? There was no judgement, it was acceptance, and this frightened me. This is what Kim thinks is going on, she doesn't really know. Kim came with a belief that I was genuinely a good person; this was the invitation. I had a belief that I was really bad. Always the fear of discovery. The Russian Doll story felt inviting, it felt like a promise. It was hopeful. I was frightened to believe in it.

The Russian Doll offered me a framework, a logical way of understanding where I was. I could understand this, but I couldn't emotionally invest in it. Feelings would emerge but I didn't know how to feel them. I didn't know what I was feeling. I could know in my head how I felt, but I couldn't feel it. Neck down I was just switched off.

Most of the time in this early part of the therapy I just felt confused. I was so worried about what Kim was thinking I could barely take notice of the story we were creating. I was managing so much. Should I look at Kim, should I not? When is it time to go? Can I come again? What if I crumble? Kim was sitting so close. I was so worried about her seeing me. My body told me the same; I was sweating and shaky. I was so nervous. My hands were squeezed into fists. My jaw was clenched. I felt rigid. When I left, I couldn't really remember what we had talked about. It felt like a dream. Intellectually we were discovering the Russian Doll, but emotionally I was chaos. It was so painful. I wanted there to be another way. I wanted to escape from the chaos. I wanted Kim to take it all away, to make me completely perfect.

I kept coming back. Part of me really wanted to come whilst another part wanted to run away. It felt powerful knowing I could stop at any time. I think in part it was this that let me keep coming back.

Upon reflection, the idea of the Russian Doll had given me a way to make sense of the person I had become. Going over and over this started to calm the chaos. It also allowed me to organise my thoughts, my feelings, my memories. They weren't so vague any more. To mix metaphors, the Russian Doll gave us the sorting office (I am laughing as I write this, as I am well known for mixing metaphors!).

I feel as though this helped me to know what was real and what was not real. Before this it had not been clear. One of my fears when I started therapy was that I did not know if I was real or not. Now I was beginning to feel real. My story was becoming more coherent.

Reflections from Kim

I returned from my trip and reconnected with Alexia. Giving her a gift seemed to overwhelm her, even though we had planned this. Deserving to be held in mind was a new experience for Alexia. She both liked it and feared it. I could see the tension, as she wanted to embrace it but feared so much that I would uncover the bad in her and it would all be lost.

We picked up where we had left off. Together we explored what Alexia could remember of growing up in foster care, the experience that had led to this, and the impact of this upon her as an adult. This was a story of emotional abuse and neglect. We also touched upon a story of sexual abuse and the trauma this had left within her. Later we would discover how lightly we touched on this. It was uncomfortable territory for both of us, but perhaps we also sensed that there was work we needed to do on other parts of Alexia's story before facing this.

As we revisited the past we were also thinking about the present. The gentle movement between the present and the past gave a rhythm and pace to the sessions which kept us moving forward.

Alexia was discovering who she was as a care-experienced adult.

She feared how others would see her. She did not want people to pity her, or to be given things that she hadn't earned because of this 'badge' of having grown up in care. She feared that being known as a 'care-leaver' would make her less good in other people's eyes. How could she not fear this, when her own eyes saw someone who was bad, undeserving of the care and attention from others?

Alexia was also exploring her relationships with her fiancé and planning her wedding. Whilst she felt she had found security within this relationship, she also feared commitment. She worried that here, too, she would not be good enough. Being 'found out' was a big theme for Alexia.

Finally, embarking on this new phase in her life inevitably meant looking back, revisiting her relationships with birth and foster family. The past and the present touched and intertwined in Alexia's life, as in our work together.

We always began in the present: Alexia would catch me up on what had been happening since we last met. She would draw this out, knowing where we were heading but delaying the inevitable for just a little while. She sat comfortably in the chair opposite me, but I could see the tension in her body. Her hands were rarely still, and she held herself just a little too rigidly. I would sit and wait, listening to her, noticing the islets of strength that she displayed as she managed the complexity of the demands on her: work, family, pets, all with their own unique need of her. Noticing, also, the waters around these islets, full of the anxieties and insecurities which came with her wherever she headed; the now familiar fears of not being good enough, of being too much for people, of not being deserving. I reflected on how hard the ordinary was for Alexia, coupled as it was with these self-doubts. I wondered about the extraordinary she was also managing within this burden.

Whilst I listened, I was also alert to that moment in the session when we would move on: the moment when Alexia was ready to move further into the difficult waters. We would swim together as Alexia started to allow herself to feel the pain, the loss, the fear that lay beneath the anxieties she was displaying. The tissues were ready as the tears flowed. I think the ease with which these tears came surprised both of us. Alexia did not cry easily, and certainly not in front of someone. Here, in this room, however, she could let go of her lifelong need to hide this emotion. I was awed by her trust in me, as she allowed herself to feel, and allowed me to share this feeling, anxiety gone as grief and loss emerged. This was a catharsis of sorts as Alexia allowed herself to feel the pain that had been buried within her for so long.

I helped Alexia by being with her. By allowing her to go where she needed with my presence holding and supporting her. I also supported Alexia by listening, helping her to make sense of what she felt. This was truly affective-reflective as we felt together and explored together. This would be a time of making linkages, noticing what she was feeling and thinking in the present and how this was inextricably linked to past experiences.

I accepted without judgement. It was not my place to try to change how she felt about herself. Acceptance was not always easy. The therapist suffers with the client. It would be easy to move us both away from this suffering through a lack of acceptance: not 'this is what you are feeling', but a focus on 'this is what you should be feeling'. Those 'shoulds' were tempting, justified by comments such as 'It is not your fault,' 'You were very little,' 'Stop blaming yourself.' This might have helped me; it would not have helped Alexia. She would have retreated back within her defences, my lack of acceptance experienced as another person in her life not able to unconditionally accept her. I was grateful to have the DDP model to guide me in this. This helped me to trust the process, giving me confidence that positive change would come when the time was right. A favourite quote by Dutch Catholic priest, professor, writer and theologian Henri Nouwen also helped me:

Let us not underestimate how hard it is to be compassionate. Compassion is hard because it requires the inner disposition to go with others to places where they are weak, vulnerable, lonely, and broken. But this is not our spontaneous response to suffering. What we desire most is to do away with suffering by fleeing from it or finding a quick cure for it. (Nouwen 2011)

Oh, how I longed to move away at times. Alexia did not deserve to feel weak, vulnerable, lonely or broken. I wanted so much more for her. Nouwen helped me to stay where Alexia needed me to be, whilst also helping me not to be too hard on myself for at times wanting to run away from this. If I could not accept these parts of Alexia, how would she be able to accept them as parts of herself, understandable parts given her early experience? I knew resilience could grow from my understanding and acceptance.

Alexia too found this difficult. Acceptance penetrated to the core of herself, and this was deeply uncomfortable. It exposed her own lack of acceptance, expressed in her need for me to help her to make the hard stuff go away. As she became aware that this was not what we were going to do in therapy, it presented her with a conflict. How could she be a 'good client' and yet reject the centre of what I was offering to her, unconditional acceptance? How could she maintain the defences she wanted to strengthen when acceptance cut right into them? I became a guide, wanted and feared by Alexia. A guide who could help her to discover acceptance for things about herself that she had little patience for. Embracing things about herself that she wanted to go away. Alexia needed to discover that she could be both vulnerable and strong, and both were okay.

The exploration we were now engaged in was very emotional for Alexia. It took her to experiences that she had previously worked hard to avoid. It tested her capacity for emotional regulation to its limits. To help with this, we did some practical work together on managing stress and anxiety. We worked together on creating a safe-place visualisation. Alexia imagined a scene where she felt safe and learnt to visualise this in some detail. When she felt stressed or overwhelmed, she could imagine herself there. Focusing on the sights and sounds she visualised was calming. We also discovered breathing exercises that worked for Alexia. She explored mindfulness. She learnt how to orientate herself, focusing on her environment, what she could see, hear, feel, taste and touch, to help her when memories became too overwhelming. Self-care was an important focus. Alexia liked to regulate through exercise and regularly attended a class.

Alexia recognised that she neglected herself at the times she most needed to take care of herself. She worked hard to change this, whilst also accepting that there were times when she couldn't do so. Change and acceptance, two opposing needs that Alexia had to reconcile. We discovered how 'black and white' Alexia was as she struggled to learn how to hold two ideas or perspectives in mind. It doesn't have to be either/or, it can be both!

The first phase of our work had felt like an infancy. During this second phase I could see Alexia growing up, learning about the world as a child, and developing the cognitive maturity to move beyond this. Moving beyond black and white was a clear reflection of this. Alexia learnt to laugh at herself for this tendency to think in absolutes. It was a laughter touched with compassion as she realised how hard she made things for herself.

Having worked therapeutically with many children, looked after and adopted, I was surprised at how fast things went with Alexia. I noticed the difference when an adult chooses therapy compared to the children who are brought by family members. At times this took my breath away. The relationship and trust-building were so much faster. I followed where Alexia led, but often found that I was leading her into slowing down this exploration, not wanting her to become too emotionally overwhelmed. I had to learn to trust her in what she could manage, so that my leads would help her deepen emotional experience and understanding. I recognised my own avoidant attachment history kicking in, as I felt a need to reduce the affective experience of what we were reflecting upon. I had to question, was this for her benefit or for mine? My own reflection and supervision were important to make sure I was supporting the therapeutic process, allowing a pace and depth that Alexia needed.

Alexia was ready to feel her experience as well as to think about it. I learnt to trust her with this and to guide her through the affective-reflective dialogues we were having together. These dialogues were the cornerstone of our conversations. They allowed us to curiously explore her experience, including the emotional aspects of this (reflect). At the same time, I provided sufficient co-regulation of the affect associated with the reflections that Alexia could experience this with me. She was able to feel the fear, pain and longings associated with her reflections, whilst gaining new meanings of these, without the shame and terror of her childhood experience. These new meanings were integrated into a coherent narrative about herself and the impact of her past experience. This allowed her story to emerge more fully.

As we were having these conversations, we started to recognise the parts of her that had developed to make things go away. We used the analogy of the Russian Doll to help us to understand this. As we explored the Russian Doll, we could see the many parts of Alexia that had helped her to survive.

We would sit together looking at a Russian Doll I had set out on the table. Therapist and client moved to the background as we became explorers together. The Russian Doll became our guide as we explored what each doll in the whole represented. Sometimes we would play with an idea about one of the dolls only to find that it didn't quite fit. We would revise our story as the doll came to represent something different. We would notice ways of being that Alexia had adopted at different parts of her life and map these onto one of the dolls.

This was a time of remembering and storytelling. Alexia would relate stories from her childhood as she remembered how she had been: stories of hiding, of running, of longing, of getting angry or of feeling nothing. Each story taught us a little more about the parts of the doll that we were exploring. We would give each doll names – Painted Doll, Empty Doll, Golden Doll, Angry Doll – recognising that these represented both parts of Alexia and a layer of defence built to protect her from her vulnerability and pain. Curiosity was high as we worked together to understand what Alexia had been and what she had needed to do. Like finding pieces of a jigsaw, each new discovery helped us to build a picture of the whole.

This was a fascinating and compelling part of the therapy for both of us. We felt like archaeologists as we discovered the layers of defence that Alexia had built in order to survive. These were times of great curiosity as we became eager to know what else we would discover.

In one session we were revisiting this. We had put the four dolls out in a row and I noticed something about the smallest doll. I picked it up to examine it more closely. We were both amazed to find a fifth doll. The fourth doll had become stuck and we thought we had found them all. The smallest, 'Baby Doll', was hidden. I loved the parallels between our metaphor and Alexia's experience. The baby part of Alexia was indeed well hidden and the hardest to embrace. Finding this doll pointed the way to what we needed to explore next.

Even at this early stage of exploring this smallest part of herself, Alexia's feelings towards it were clear. She hated it. Our curiosity about this part was tinged with Alexia's animosity. This was the part of herself that she most blamed. If it hadn't been so weak and helpless, so vulnerable, all would have been well. She would have been acceptable to her mother; the abuse and neglect would not have happened. Alexia's core belief was full of self-blame, and this was most clear when we thought about Baby Doll. Her self-blame went right back to the beginning of her life.

I could understand this intellectually. Alexia still held on to the hope for an unconditional mother. If she moved the blame from self to mother, then this hope died. By maintaining a belief that it was her fault, Alexia could hold on to a hope that if she could be better, less vulnerable, less needy, more perfect, then unconditional love might still be hers. This was what the defences were all about. This is why she had become Painted Doll.

Understanding this was easier than sitting with it. My heart ached that Alexia could not see herself as I could see her. That she could not allow herself to feel vulnerable, confident that others would care for her. That she could not admire her strength, wisdom and compassion. Alexia was playing a blame game and pointing the finger at herself.

It wasn't about attributing blame; all the players in this particular drama had their own stories. I needed to help Alexia to find understanding. In reflecting on her feelings for Baby Doll we could understand why Alexia had developed the defences that she had. The self-blame and its role in protecting her made sense to us. Alexia was not yet ready to accept the vulnerability that Baby Doll represented, but she could begin to understand it. Curiosity was helping us to understand the Russian Doll, in all its parts, and why they had developed.

Curiosity was high, but affective arousal was never far away. This was also an emotional journey as we travelled from outside in, understanding each defence in turn and discovering what was being hidden at each layer. As we came to understand what the different dolls represented, Alexia would embrace the vulnerability that lay under the defence. This got harder the further back we went. Alexia was aware of intense shame at her feelings of not being good enough, of not deserving things and of fears that she would be 'found out'. Curiosity would subside as Alexia became absorbed in feelings and the fears accompanying them. She would sit back in the chair, crying quietly, almost shrinking into herself. I would sit quietly with her, expressing empathy for how hard this was and understanding for why she carried these fears. Alexia would absorb my acceptance. I would see her body relax as she settled more deeply into the chair. A calmness would descend. Sometimes this would lead to more memories, more thoughts. Sometimes it would be enough; we would chat for a while, about this and that, until Alexia felt ready to leave.

The past continued to be reflected in the present. This was a time when much attention was on Alexia, as bride to be. Alexia found being with people difficult, as she needed to please everyone. The more people she was with, the harder this was to do. She was excited for her wedding but also intensely embarrassed by the attention. She felt undeserving of this attention. She would seek to prove this to herself. For example, she would search out disappointments in gifts, to find a flaw, however small, to prove to herself that she wasn't good enough.

It was startling at times to find similarities with Alexia. Therapy was truly a two-way process, as I learnt about myself through my increased understanding of Alexia. I could recognise the same difficulties and challenges in my own life. I too sought flaws in gifts. I too found being with people tiring because of my need to please. I had to reflect on whether to share this. Would it be helpful to Alexia to know I understood some of her experience because it was also my own? I decided it would, but was careful to keep the focus on her experience rather than my own whilst sharing. I needed to take my own therapeutic needs elsewhere.

This was an intense piece of work. Alexia still had to face exploring Baby Doll, whilst needing to absorb all the work we had been doing with the other dolls. Helpfully, we had a natural break as I was going away for another few weeks. This would give Alexia some time and space before moving forward again.

As before when I went away, Alexia needed a way of knowing I was holding her in mind. She still could not trust that this would happen. During our first break we had agreed that I would bring back a gift for her. When we were planning for this second break Alexia suggested that I write a therapeutic story which I could share with her whilst I was away. She agreed to provide me with some reflections to guide this story, and in this way we would be writing it together; a connection across the world. It was a lovely idea and would indeed demonstrate the invisible string that maintained a connection between us even when apart (Karst & Stevenson 2001). The fact that Alexia requested this revealed the progress she was making; she had confidence that I would hold her in mind long enough to write the story.

I ended up writing two stories. My first story, 'Finding Me', was written in the first person based upon the co-created story about Alexia's childhood and experiences that arose from our reflections within the sessions. I used many of Alexia's own words and phrases in writing this story. This was the biggest 'talking for' her that I attempted. Telling the story we had discovered from her perspective was emotional for me. Reading it could potentially be an emotionally overwhelming experience for Alexia. I reflected upon this and decided that I would not share this story by email. I wanted to be with Alexia when she heard it. I subsequently added to this story as we continued to work together. This is the story that is presented in segments at the beginning of the chapters. It provides a framework for our reflections of the therapy.

The story I ultimately shared at a distance was a metaphorical story; the metaphor provided some distance that would reduce the emotional intensity. I wanted Alexia to experience it at both an affective and reflective level without becoming emotionally overwhelmed. The Russian Doll was an obvious metaphor for me to draw upon. We include this story at the end of this chapter.

In discovering the Russian Doll, we had opened a lot of emotional experience for Alexia. She had to choose whether to live with the vulnerability that was emerging or not. We had to discover the strengths that this also brought. This would be the third phase of our work, as Alexia searched for a healthier way to be.

The Russian Doll

The Russian Doll is a set of wooden nesting dolls of decreasing size so that they stack into one doll. It is also known as a Matryoshka Doll. This name comes from the Russian word 'matryoshka' (матрёшка), which literally means 'little matron': a diminutive form for a Russian female. The traditional Russian Doll is painted to represent this. The outer layer is a woman dressed in a sarafan: a long and shapeless traditional Russian peasant jumper dress.

Once upon a time there was a doll. She was the most beautiful painted doll that you can imagine. She lived in a painted doll's house, as beautiful as herself. All those who saw her admired her. The doll lived alone. No-one was quite sure of her age. She appeared timeless, as if she had lived on Earth for many years. And yet, sometimes, if you caught sight of her out of the corner of your eye, you would wonder, 'Oh, but she is just a child after all.' You look again more fully and doubt yourself: 'No, she is grown up. I was wrong.'

This doll was liked by all who met her. She was kind and she was helpful. Nothing was too much trouble. She loved to take care of others. She delighted in pleasing them. She asked nothing in return. She was described as 'golden', a gem amongst them. All who knew her loved her. Sometimes she retreated into her house for a time, and then they felt sad. They called to her to come back to them. She always responded, joining them again, a smile on her face.

Unbeknown to these people, who relied so much on the doll, she had a secret. A deep sadness lay within her, unseen by anyone and ignored by her. She knew that she was just a painted doll. Inside she felt empty. She wasn't 'golden'. She was nothing. She was nameless.

The doll worked hard to keep the secret hidden, but sometimes she was so tired. It became more difficult. She would retreat into her empty house for a time. She would experience headaches, her stomach hurt, it even felt hard to breathe. She longed for someone to come to her, to notice how she suffered. No-one came. She longed to live in a village where there was no sadness. Bearing sadness alone was beyond unbearable; better not to feel. The doll resolved to do better. She berated herself for her weakness. She would not be sad. She would not be ill. She would not need anyone. She heard them calling for her. With a heavy heart, and a brave smile, she went to them again.

And thus it continued, day after day, year after year. The doll buried the sadness and the longing deep within her. She strived to be the person that other people wanted of her.

Who knows how long this would have continued if a young man had not entered her life? He was new to the village, and the doll looked at him and admired him. He smiled shyly at her and she smiled back. A friendship developed. Sometimes they walked along the riverside, talking together. Something awoke inside of the doll. This frightened her. She wanted it gone, but she wanted her friend.

Others noticed the developing friendship. They did not like it. How dare he? She was their doll. They didn't want him taking her from them. How would she be there to help them if she was with him? The doll was conflicted. She wanted to please the villagers. She wanted to please him. She didn't know what to do. She retreated into her empty house. A great sadness filled the emptiness within her. The doll didn't like this. She wanted to be empty again. When they called to her she called angrily to tell them to leave her alone. More feelings, what was happening? She felt that she was breaking apart.

The young man came to her. The doll didn't know what to do. She called him to her. She told him to go away. He was patient. He told her it was okay. He would wait for her.

It was at her lowest ebb, not knowing what to do, that she called out, 'Help me.' She expected no answer. Who had ever come when she called? She berated herself for being so foolish. She would have to sort this out. This would not do.

Her friend came to her. She did not want him to see her like this. She told him to go away. He took her by the hands and looked deep into her eyes. The doll was afraid. He would notice that she was painted, empty. Worse, he might see she was bad. He would not want to be her friend any more.

Quietly he spoke to her. 'I know you are a painted doll, but I believe you are so much more. You need to go on a journey. Answer the knock. I will wait for you.' He left her then, but reminded her as he walked away, 'Answer the knock, go where it takes you. Believe I will never be far away. Believe that I will wait for you.'

The doll was alone, and frightened. She feared what her friend had seen. He would not care for her now. She didn't understand what he had said to her. She only knew he had gone away. The villagers were angry, they left her alone. She didn't know what to do. Then she heard a quiet knocking at the door. The doll hid, frightened.

The knocking continued, gentle but persistent. The doll remembered her friend's words. Slowly, hesitantly, she opened the door. 'Hello Matryoshka, I am here to help you.' The doll was confused: 'That isn't my name. Why do you call me that?'

The Wise Lady smiled. 'You need a name if you are to discover you are real. It is my name for you. I think it suits you very well. Are you ready?'

And so, the journey began.

The Wise Lady and the doll travelled far and wide. They fell into a rhythm and the doll found that she did not feel so alone, so frightened. Despite herself, she began talking. She told of her fear. She was a painted doll born from a painted doll. She was empty, all she could do was please others. She feared discovery. If they found her out she would have nothing left.

The Wise Lady smiled. 'You are being so brave. You feel empty but look at what I can see. You love, you fear, you want. I don't see an empty doll; I see a living girl who is frightened of looking into the emptiness. Will you look with me?'

The girl considered; she felt a tiny spark of hope: 'What will I see?' she asked.

The Wise Lady looked at her kindly. 'You will see things that frighten you, make you angry, and make you sad. But you won't see emptiness.'

'Why would I want to see those things?' asked the girl. 'Won't they hurt me? Won't they weaken me? I don't want to feel frightened, angry or sad. Why should I look?'

The Wise Lady looked at Matryoshka with compassion. 'I know this is hard, but I want you to trust me. You feel empty and this is weakening you. Feel the fear, anger and sadness. Be brave. This will make you stronger.'

'How will it make me stronger?' puzzled the girl. 'Can't I feel nice things, happy things? Why do I have to be full of such horrible feelings? Why can't you help me make them go away?'

'You need to feel all your feelings, nice and not so nice,' said the Wise Lady. 'Be patient. You have hidden from feelings for so long. It has split you into parts that you have hidden away. That is why you are empty. You ran from fear, anger and sadness. You lost all your feelings along the way. Happiness, joy, comfort, they don't feel real for you either. You need to reclaim all your feelings, to look at them and know them, to accept that they are not right nor wrong. This is so hard for you. You feel bad, contaminated by feelings that just are. This is the journey you must make. Then you will feel real and whole again. You are a **Russian Doll**. There is so much more inside. The outer doll is painted but you will find your authentic self. Once **Painted Doll** finds the other dolls you will discover who you really are.'

The girl listened, and though she dreaded what she was told, something told her that this was right. This was her journey. She felt some courage rise inside her. She would do this, and the lady would help her. Painted Doll would look inside herself and reclaim what she had buried within her. 'Who shall I meet first?' she asked.

'You have met one already,' the Wise Lady replied. 'I found her in your empty house. **Empty Doll** was there. You stepped out of hiding and revealed her to me, you accepted her. You are already more than you were, Matryoshka. You have a name. Soon we will meet the next doll.'

The next day dawned bright and sunny. They set off at a

brisk pace, journeying together. They fell into a rhythm, walking, resting, feeding, sleeping. Sometimes they talked. Sometimes they were silent, comfortable in each other's company.

One day they reached a town, not unlike the town where Painted Doll lived. As they walked through it the Wise Lady said that they would rest a while and take some food. A girl came forward and offered to help them. She took them to an inn and bade them rest whilst she prepared food for them. Matryoshka watched the girl. She was merry and gay. Others called out to her, demanding this and that. She answered each with a smile as she met their requests.

'Sit with us,' said Matryoshka. 'You must be weary.'

The girl just laughed. 'No, I cannot sit. Look at everyone, I must take care of them. No, I will not sit.'

'Who are you?' asked Matryoshka.

'Don't you recognise me?' she replied. 'I am **Golden Doll**.'

And then Matryoshka understood, and she was afraid. 'I hate that name,' she said. 'Everyone thinks I am golden, but I am not. I am just me. Why can't they see? Why don't they know how sad I am underneath the painted smile? Why, just once, couldn't they take care of me?'

As she spoke, the inn and all the people disappeared. It left just the three of them. Golden Doll fell with exhaustion. Gently the Wise Lady went to her and lifted her up. She gave her to Matryoshka. 'You are so strong,' Matryoshka said, 'and so alone. I am here now, come to me. I will look after you.'

'But I like taking care of others,' protested Golden Doll.

'You still can,' smiled the Wise Lady. 'Let Matryoshka help you, as you are helping her. Learn that you can let others care for you as well.'

Matryoshka felt her strength increase as Golden Doll joined Empty Doll inside her. She didn't need to be empty or golden any more, just herself.

The journey continued. Matryoshka was a little apprehensive.

Facing Empty Doll and Golden Doll was hard, but she had done it. She was able to embrace and accept these parts of herself. Whilst she hated other people's responses to them because of what they missed, she could see how they had helped her. She had the sense that further in it was going to be more difficult. She feared what she would find, and what it would reveal about herself.

One day, as the afternoon was drawing to a close, and they were both feeling tired, they arrived at another town. They ate and rested and then the Wise Lady suggested a walk. They hadn't gone far when they heard a commotion ahead. A child, maybe five years old, was shouting as if her life depended on it: 'I won't, you can't make me!' Matryoshka watched as the adults tried to appease her. Nothing seemed to help. The child glared at them all, lashing out at the children closest to her. They separated her and sat her by herself. As soon as they left her the child made herself sick. The adults rushed back to her. She laughed as she ran away.

Matryoshka was appalled. What was wrong with the child? Where had all that anger come from?

'Go to her,' the Wise Lady said.

'Go to her?' replied Matryoshka. 'You can't mean it? Surely this child has nothing to do with me?' But in her heart, she knew she was wrong. This child was **Angry Doll** and had everything to do with her. She recognised the strong, powerful feelings that she had buried so long ago. Golden Doll had helped her to make them go away. 'I don't know if I can do this,' she protested, but she sought out the child all the same. As she drew near, she found her, alone and sobbing. Her heart went out to her.

'Go away,' shouted Angry Doll, wiping all trace of tears from her face. 'Leave me alone. I don't need your help.'

Matryoshka stepped back, propelled by the force of the doll's anger. The empathy she had felt a moment ago vanished as she experienced the hurt of the doll's rejection of her. She wasn't sure what to do next. She didn't want to experience this anger for herself.

The Wise Lady spoke to her. 'You need the anger, just as you need the caring parts. They are all a part of you. Anger brings strength if it is tempered with wisdom. Remember that underneath all that fury is a sad and frightened doll. She needs you although she will never admit it. Stay close, take it slow.'

Every instinct in Matryoshka said to turn and walk away, but she had come so far. It took all her courage to move forward and to sit close to where the doll was still shouting at her. Slowly, as she watched the small doll, some of the feelings she had experienced long ago returned to her. She had been so hurt by those she trusted. She recognised the need to feel strong and powerful. To keep people noticing her without letting them in. With intensity and energy in her voice she spoke out loud. 'She is so brave and strong. She is doing this all by herself. She doesn't want me near, why would she? I will just let her down like everyone else. I will hurt her too. How could she expect any different?' As she talked, she noticed the doll quieten, although she remained tense, vigilant, ready to fight her at any moment. They stayed like this for a long time, the doll alternating bouts of anger with quieter vigilance.

Finally, it was as if the fight had left Angry Doll. She crept closer to Matryoshka. Matryoshka talked quietly and softly now. She talked of the sadness when it feels like no-one loves you. She talked of the horror when those you love act in ways that hurt you. She talked of the fear that you are so bad that bad things will always happen to you and everyone will abandon you in the end. She talked of the anger that seems the only way to feel safe. She talked of the bravery it takes to stay angry all the time.

'How do you know?' asked the doll. 'How do you know that is how I feel?'

Matryoshka smiled. 'You and I are the same,' she said. 'I had just forgotten it for a while.'

Angry Doll snuggled into Matryoshka. She joined Empty Doll and Golden Doll. Matryoshka felt anger enter her. 'Will I cope?'

she asked the Wise Lady. 'Will I be able to manage these strong feelings? Am I strong enough?'

'Most of the time,' the Wise Lady replied. 'They will help you to get what you need. Remember, anger isn't bad, you just need to find a way to express it safely. Sometimes it will be hard. You will feel overwhelmed. You will have to find a way to deal with that too.'

The next few weeks were spent quietly, as Matryoshka absorbed all that had happened. She needed to get used to the new feelings she was allowing herself to experience. This was a peaceful time for the two of them. Quietly the Wise Lady took care of Matryoshka, who in turn was learning to let her. Always, though, there remained a fear inside of her, insistent and troubling. What if the Wise Lady was wrong? What if she couldn't cope? What if she really was bad? Would she be found out? Would she lose everything after all?

The Wise Lady understood. 'These are troubling worries, but they are understandable. You have lived with these fears for a long time. I will take care of you as you learn to love yourself. You are many things, Matryoshka, they are all parts of you. It is not black and white; live with the colours that are you.'

Matryoshka was not in a hurry for this time to end. She knew there was a greater challenge ahead and she dreaded this one most of all. But the day came when they had to set out once more.

This time the way was difficult. They had to find paths and cross streams. The Wise Lady guided them steadily. Her calm confidence helped to soothe Matryoshka's troubled mind. This continued for many weeks.

One day they came across some turbulent water and looked for a crossing place. They found some stepping stones, wet and slippery. Cautiously Matryoshka made her way across, making sure of each step as she went. As she reached the far side her attention was drawn to something caught in the reeds. She reached out and touched a wicker basket. Drawing it towards her she was horrified to find a baby inside. She looked around. 'Where is the mother? How could she leave her baby like this?'

'She comes, and she goes,' the Wise Lady replied. 'She is kind and she is cruel. She gives but demands much in return. This is **Baby Doll.**'

Between them they lifted the basket onto the bank. 'Now what?' asked Matryoshka.

'You will take care of her,' said the Wise Lady.

This was too much. Matryoshka felt anger rising within her. 'I can't do it. Look at her. She is weak and vulnerable. No, not this time.' Matryoshka moved away and sat hugging herself. This is too hard. This is where it all began. If she wasn't so helpless, so unlovable, she wouldn't have been abandoned like this. It is her fault. She needs to grow up, stop needing so much.

The Wise Lady sat with her. She absorbed the strong feelings and did not judge the harsh words.

'I am bad, I am bad,' moaned Matryoshka.

'You feel bad because you need. It is so hard to feel vulnerable, lost and lonely.' The Wise Lady spoke quietly and compassionately. 'You fear my judgement, but you judge yourself so harshly. You are so little; how could you not feel it is your fault? All you wanted was a mother to love you unconditionally. It is not so much to ask for.'

Then Matryoshka felt anger towards the mother who could have given her what she needed, but didn't. This anger joined the anger towards herself. This was a hard time for Matryoshka, accepting her vulnerability, trying to forgive those who had hurt her so much, whilst living with the anger that kept returning. Without the Wise Lady to support and guide her it would have been impossible.

Finally, Matryoshka was ready. She went back to the baby. She picked her up and cradled her. She spoke softly: 'I am sorry I was angry with you. It is not your fault. You are tiny, how could you do anything else? Come to me. I need you. Teach me how to need again.'

This was the hardest of all. To absorb the weak, helpless feelings. Feelings that had been denied for the longest time. Sometimes Matryoshka found herself getting angry. She wanted to be self-reliant again. She wanted to take care of others and not feel so dependent. She complained to the Wise Lady: 'I thought you would help me to become a different person by making all the difficult stuff go away. This is so much harder. I feel bad, contaminated. How can I accept these parts of me?'

And yet somehow Matryoshka did. With the help of the Wise Lady she learnt to live with the difficult feelings. There were setbacks, difficult days. She was learning to be, all over again. The world felt unsteady, wobbly; it felt safer to retreat to the familiar again, but somehow she found the strength to keep going.

And so, they returned to where it all started. A painted doll's house for a painted doll. Matryoshka pushed open the door fearing the loneliness and emptiness within. But everything had changed! It was homely and welcoming, full of warmth and love. A real house.

And he was waiting there for her. Gently he took her by the hand and guided her to the mirror. 'Look,' he said. 'The Painted Doll has gone. You are a living, breathing, whole person. Welcome back.'

'I still have a long way to go,' warned Matryoshka. 'This is all so new. I am a baby, a child, an adult. I need to rediscover my childhood. Sometimes I will be angry. Sometimes I will withdraw. Will you be patient with me? Will I wear you out?'

He took her in his arms. 'We will just have to see, won't we? No-one knows the future, but don't predict it based on the past, Matryoshka. Perhaps trust is the hardest feeling of them all.'

Chapter 4

STRIVING FOR HEALTH: PAINTED DOLL BECOMES REAL

FINDING ME

I don't want to be the weak vulnerable baby. I don't want to be the angry small child. I don't want to be the golden child. I am tired of trying to be empty. I don't want to be painted any more. I want to be me, an authentic person, not vulnerable, not angry, not golden, not empty, not painted, just me. I fear the real me is full of badness. I am afraid to find it. Will I be acceptable to you if I can find my authentic self? I need to go slowly.

It is a time of big change for me. I am about to be married. I am seeking a career. Am I old enough for all this? We meet together. I trust you slowly. I reveal myself slowly. I have to be so brave, take risks, let you see the me I fear is inside. Bit by bit we find a me I was not expecting, not good, not bad, just me. I can only come to this slowly. Test each part of me, piece by piece.

First, I have to understand the me I think I know. I fear in finding this 'me' I will lose you. You are constant, accepting, not judging the parts of me that I judge so fiercely.

I am a private person. I do not trust easily. People don't know me, can't read me. This is how I keep myself hidden from view. I fear I will be unacceptable to others if they see who I am. I so fear being found out, losing everything. I won't cry in front of others. I won't get angry. I will please.

It is so exhausting. Even with him, the person I am closer to than I have ever been with anyone, the person I will share my life with, I fear. I reveal myself in bits, and then withdraw.

Will you abandon me too? I long for unconditional love. I realise I have longed for this all my life. I am so lonely without it.

I am a controlling person, even the parts that others approve of are another way of being in charge. I feel this is bad, but you help me to see it is heroic. It has kept me alive.

I ask for nothing from others. I take care of them. I am helpful. I keep my own needs hidden. I reveal no emotion. People think they know me, but they only see Painted Doll.

Only two people see the chips in the paint, see glimpses of the real me hidden in the emptiness. Husband and therapist.

I explore these glimpses in therapy, but I am so frightened. Do not abandon me. I am tired of always being the grown up. I lost my childhood. Can I be a child with you?

I want to see myself through the eyes of others. The real me, the authentic me. How do I know what is real? Can I trust my own sense of self? I live in a world of colours but see in black and white. You are good, I am bad. You will love me; you will hate me. You tell me there is an in between. I cannot see it. You tell me we will discover the colours together. I want to lose parts of myself. You tell me to accept. How can I accept what I fear and hate?

Reflections from Alexia

A lot of things were happening in my life during this time that felt monumental: getting married, finding a new job. I had a sense that I wanted to approach these differently. I was beginning to see that maybe it was okay to put my needs first. Our wedding was a time to test this way of being. I was trying on new shoes and watching people's reactions. For the first time in my life I felt able to challenge others in my family and do what felt right for Andrew and me, despite the anger and rejection that it might cause. I stuck firm, knowing that marrying Andrew was truly what I wanted, whereas previously I would have been swayed by the needs of others. I was beginning to experiment with who my authentic self was. Sometimes this felt confusing. Was this really me? Am I just exchanging one mask for another? It was really important that I could talk to Kim about this. She became a guide, helping me to trust that I was on the right track. I would find myself being swept along by others and their opinions of what was right or wrong. Kim would help me to reflect on what I needed. Kim held my needs for me and could direct me when I lost sight of them.

There was also a deeper meaning to this. We began to think about why I had never had my needs met. This confronted the trauma and loss and its impact on me. I felt unsure. Was it okay to see myself as not at fault? What would that mean for my relationships with others? I feared who I would lose in this process. My foster carers and my siblings were at the forefront of my mind. Would I be acceptable to them if I was different; if I changed? I felt uncertain about whether it was worth the risk. This was a critical point. Should I keep going forwards or turn back? I was having a lot of bad dreams during this time. I think they were a reflection of how difficult this was for me.

It was also hard to revisit my early experience when I remembered so little. Reading my notes helped but was also frustrating.

So much of my life was blacked out! I was surprised at schoolteachers noticing that I was angry as a five-year-old. I knew that I had not displayed anger in my second and last foster home. My foster parents have told me that they never saw me angry. What had happened to the angry child? There is so much unknown. I have bodily experiences but few memories, and so few facts. I have to rely on my sense of what happened, never sure if this relates to true happenings or not.

Some memories are clearer. I can remember being in hospital for a minor operation when I was four and being terrified when I was being held down for the general anaesthetic. I was angry then, fighting to get them off me. Other experiences, sometimes from very young, are much hazier. Even at my birth I feel like my mother screamed for me to be taken away. I think that this is the beginning of anger being dangerous and being so closely linked with fears of abandonment. My mother was a tiger who could destroy me. I was something awful and she wanted me taken away. I don't know if this is based on any 'true' events, but this is what my gut tells me, and I have learnt to trust it. What it is telling me is worth paying attention to.

As we explored the Russian Doll it was these sensations even more than the concrete memories that helped us to make sense of these discovered parts of myself. Baby Doll was truly vulnerable and Angry Doll represented a danger from which Golden Doll had to emerge.

Kim wrote two stories for this part of the therapy. She had gone away with the promise of writing a story and then told me that there were two. My first thought was disbelief that I had got two whole stories. I couldn't quite believe that I had two just for me.

Kim sent me 'The Russian Doll' by email so I could read it whilst she was away. Reading it, I couldn't believe how well Kim knew me. For the first time there was a reason for what had happened, and not because I had done something wrong. For the first time I could think maybe it wasn't my fault – it offered me a different story to the one I had for myself. A story that was kind, accepting, compassionate and gentle. It felt as if I had a sense of who I was. Although we had figured this out together, exploring each part of the story across many therapy sessions, this was the first time it had all been brought together. It was a retelling of the story that we had put together bit by bit.

When Kim returned, she read the 'Finding Me' story to me. This story felt different because Kim had given me a voice so that I could be heard. This was much more emotionally intense. Kim would stop frequently to check in with me; to check that I wasn't overwhelmed. It was hard to look at her. I felt shy that someone knew me so well. I was being properly seen. It was like when a parent looks at an infant knowing she can do no wrong. Nothing about me was seen as bad or mad; there was no judgement. I was being given a sense that I was my own person, with my own space. I had my own right to exist.

Reflections from Kim

As we explored the Russian Doll, Alexia was gaining an understanding of what was needed if she was to achieve her goals. She wanted to find her real self, to feel authentic. To achieve this, she would need to integrate the experience of loss and trauma. Far from perfecting ways to avoid emotional experience, Alexia was learning that she needed to embrace it. To achieve authenticity Alexia would have to discover why she had developed the defences we were exploring, and to understand the fears underlying these. Alexia needed the courage to face what she had been hiding from all her life: her vulnerability.

Alexia needed to experience my non-judgement and acceptance before she could find this acceptance for herself. Her fear of being 'found out' was very high. We explored our differing goals for therapy, hers to make things go away and mine to help her towards acceptance. Alexia hated the vulnerable, angry, needy parts of herself. She saw these as the cause of all her problems. She believed she had been a bad infant and naughty child and that this had denied her the love and care she needed. She could not see how she could accept these parts of herself when they had caused her so much loss and pain. My acceptance had to stretch to this as well, much as I wanted it to be different for her. This was how Alexia felt; these were her beliefs. I did not judge these. I did, however, hold hope that she would not always feel this way; that she would come to different beliefs in time.

I have struggled with the idea of hope and its place in therapy. Alexia taught me that hope is an experience that can be a burden when misplaced, containing as it does expectations for things to be different. I thought that we needed to find a balance between hope and acceptance. I feared that without hope, acceptance would lead us to be stuck without progress. I offered hope as a path to follow. I wanted Alexia's trust in me to lead her along this path.

In discussing this with Dan Hughes, he suggested that acceptance contains its own way forward, found through the curiosity we hold which helps us to discover the person underneath the problems, and who existed before the trauma. He suggested that as we explored Alexia's traumatic experience, we were also creating an awareness of moving forward in a healthier way; the actualising tendency that Carl Rogers writes about.

I wonder now if it is not a balance between hope and acceptance that I was trying to find, but a way of holding onto acceptance when experiencing Alexia's inner life, which was so painful for me to bear. I wanted it to be different. In the Introduction, Alexia describes the tiny spark of hope that brought her into therapy with me. She did not want a big spark, which would add pressure for a change she was not ready for. I was, however, in danger of finding this big spark of hope, compromising the acceptance that was essential for Alexia if she was to find her way forward. Hope: such a little word, but if weighted with expectation, it reduces the experience of feeling accepted. I learnt that if hope gets in the way of acceptance it will be unhelpful. Hope is helpful when it is found within a trust in the process, as encouraged within the DDP model.

We began by co-creating Alexia's story together, discovering meaning through the metaphor of the Russian Doll. As we learnt about the defences, and how strongly she had built them up, we discovered layers of grief and loss underneath them. We also discovered that Alexia held a lot of anger and frustration that she had not been strong enough; that she had been vulnerable. Whilst accepting these feelings, she also had to face another truth. Maybe it was not her fault; maybe she was a young, defenceless infant who needed to be cared for. Maybe she was good enough. If she accepted this then she had to face the grief and loss of a mother for whom she had always sought. In embracing herself she lost the possibility of the mother. We realised how much the defence of Golden Doll was about preserving an idea of idealised mother. Alexia strove to be good enough for this mother to unconditionally accept her. This was a hard moment in therapy, when Alexia realised that to achieve her goal, to become authentic, she would have to lose the hope that had sustained the defences throughout her childhood. Hope, there is that word again; this time in a false form. In finding herself she would also be losing something she longed for. She needed to grieve for the mother she never had. Not only was she accepting her own vulnerability, but also having to accept her birth mother's vulnerability.

This was an emotional experience for both of us. I needed to maintain a high level of safety as Alexia managed the conflicting emotions that this exploration aroused. DDP was my guide and gave me a way of being with Alexia. Central within this was the attitude of PACE. This was my anchor. We joined together in curiosity (C), co-creating a narrative of how Alexia had survived a childhood within which her needs were not met. Acceptance (A) and empathy (E) provided the co-regulation Alexia needed to sit with the emotion that was emerging. Playfulness (P) made all this bearable, as we found joy and moments of fun in our relationship.

This was a deeply intersubjective process. I maintained an emotional connection with Alexia, as the foundation to our relationship. I privileged this connection above any technique that therapy required. Without this connection, technique would be unhelpful. The intersubjective relationship helped my intuition. It guided me in when to lead and when to follow. It gave me an instinctive feel for what Alexia could cope with at any moment, allowing us to gently challenge some of her truths, knowing when to dip into the past and when to stay in the present; when to move to some work confronting the fears; when to stay with lighter, easier themes.

Intersubjectivity meant that I was influenced by Alexia's experience. I reflected this experience back to her. This allowed Alexia to be influenced by me. New meanings emerged from this reciprocal process of being open to the influence of the other. Therapy was a collaborative process of exploration, understanding and change. As I experienced Alexia's story, our intersubjective connection allowed her to respond to my experience. This in turn changed her own experience of her story. As I experienced Alexia, as intelligent, delightful, courageous, funny, lovable and deserving, she responded to my experience and slowly her own experience of herself changed.

This was not an easy process. Change is deeply uncomfortable. Alexia trusted me, but what if I was wrong? What if we would discover the rot at the core of her? Sometimes it felt safer to stay as she was. Witnessing my acceptance and compassion towards those parts of herself she most feared felt to Alexia like her undoing. She could no longer maintain the defence of hiding these parts, making them go away. This, however, began the healing. As she experienced my acceptance, Alexia described herself as feeling calmer. Our relationship provided co-regulation, helping her to manage the uncomfortable. She was able to engage in co-creating her story with me. She was moving from a story of terror and shame towards one of hope and healing.

Understanding for Alexia also came from another source, parallel to our work together. She was finally accessing her own records and was able to fill in some of the gaps in her understanding about her childhood experience. Alexia chose to read these notes alone and then we would talk about them during our sessions. Despite her intense frustration at how much of the record was redacted, she was able to view herself through the eyes of others.

This exploration of her records paralleled Alexia's experience of my acceptance for the child she was. I think the reading of these notes helped her to develop her own acceptance and compassion for a little girl who was clearly working hard to survive. Alexia was a witness to her younger self through the eyes of those writing the notes. She recognised how they initially witnessed an angry, troubled child, evoking their concern. As she grew older Alexia could also see how good she had become at fooling everyone into thinking she was now okay. She experienced sadness that no-one appeared to recognise how troubled she still was; how much she was hurting. Alexia wished that someone had seen this but also recognised how hard she had worked to make sure that this didn't happen.

Chapter 5

FINDING
ROOTS AND WINGS

FINDING ME

I want to fly, soar into a world of confidence and maturity. Leave behind the weak and the vulnerable parts of myself. I will be fully self-reliant. You tell me I will be lost. You help me to see that I also need roots. This frightens me. Independence is seductive, dependence fills me with dread. And yet I notice, deep inside, a longing. A longing to show my need, to be taken care of, to be loved unconditionally. I acknowledge this need within me, but it is a knowledge filled with sadness. I grieve for the unconditional mother I never had.

I marry. I cannot keep myself hidden here. Intimacy is new. I embrace it but have to hide from it at times. It feels good to be supported in this journey. It feels terrifying. What if I wear him out? What if he discovers I am not acceptable to him?

I seek a different job, one where I am supported, offered a secure base. I realise how much I felt safer without this, but how dangerous to live without a secure base. Self-reliance comes with a cost: if I get it wrong there will be no-one to help me. Now I have help but I am scared. I have to trust in dependency. You will see me. What if you find me wanting? What if I am unacceptable to you? I am safer than I have ever been, but it feels so dangerous.

These are the contradictions I must come to terms with, as I discover both roots and wings. I realise that there are parts of myself that I do not like. I want them to go away. I have hidden them in the empty painted room. My false self is beautiful, but it is just paint. I no longer try to hide behind this false self. I learn that I can't lose parts of myself because they are unacceptable to me. I have to trust and learn that they are not unacceptable to you.

I started this journey to become a different person. I wanted all the difficult stuff to go away. You told me that I need to accept who I am and to find peace with what has happened to me. The idea of acceptance makes me grimace. How can I accept the bad, contaminated parts of me? You ask me to find compassion for myself and the difficult experiences that I have had to endure.

I understand the fragmented parts of myself, but it is not enough. Sometimes I think myself out of feeling it. I am working so hard to try and figure this all out. Acceptance means going beyond understanding. I need to have empathy for these part selves. You ask me to cradle the vulnerable baby, embrace the angry child, and love the golden child. Only in this way will I fill up the empty self. Only in this way can painted become real. Do I know who I really am? Am I more than the sum of these? They all worked so hard to keep me safe; in accepting them, will I find me?

Reflections from Alexia

As therapy continued, I found that I became more aware of the needs I held within me; needs I had learnt to ignore. The biggest change I remember was feeling really angry when I didn't feel my needs were being met in day-to-day life. I was also beginning to read my records and I was noticing this theme from when I was tiny. I felt angry that I had been missed. Why had no-one noticed the needs I carried buried within me?

It felt new to feel this way. Having denied dependence for so long, I now couldn't get enough of it. This need was insatiable. I was jealous of the other people that Kim supported. I wanted her all to myself. This made me feel childish. I worried that I was too much. Alongside this was always the dread. Was I asking too much? Asking for anything felt selfish. And if it wasn't selfish surely I would wear the others out? I had minimised my needs for so long. People had barely looked after me when I had no needs; how on earth could they cope if I started to ask for things? I needed and I feared at the same time. Needing roots to fly felt like a contradiction. I knew how to fly solo, now I had to learn how to fly with others. I had a lot of confusion. I couldn't believe that anyone with needs could be acceptable. Therapy awoke the needs within me. Along with this a sense of anger. It was red hot. Why hadn't I been taken care of? Why did I have to make these needs go away? Why did nobody notice me?

Reflections from Kim

Working with dependence and independence gives the therapist a challenge. We have to solve the dilemma of supporting needed dependence without either encouraging an unhealthy dependency or strengthening an unhealthy independence. Alexia had an unhealthy independence. I needed to help her to feel comfortable being dependent so that she could grow into healthy independence. As the well-known quote attributed to a wise woman expresses, we needed to find Alexia's roots and wings: 'A wise woman once said to me that there are only two lasting bequests we can hope to give our children. One of these she said is roots, the other, wings' (Hodding Carter 1953).

There was a danger in helping Alexia to discover safe dependency. The pull to be the mother to Alexia's younger selves was strong. She was grieving for a mother that she had never had and within this grief there was an invitation to fill the gap. This challenged my own attachment history; as with Alexia, nurturing others was so much easier than nurturing myself.

There were two elements that increased this pull on me. First, I recognised many of Alexia's ways of coping in myself. Whilst I had not had the abusive and traumatic experience that she had, my experience of growing up with a depressed mother had also led to a tendency towards self-reliance and a view of myself as undeserving. Second, our respective ages lent themselves to a mother-daughter-type relationship, and indeed Alexia was roughly the same age as my own daughter. I needed to remain reflective about the impulse I recognised in myself to 'adopt' Alexia as a daughter. Conversely, in an effort to avoid this possibility, I was in danger of encouraging independence at the cost of needed dependence. Finding the balancing point between dependence and independence was something we both needed to do.

Alexia struggled with dependency. Her self-reliance drove her independence, and finding a secure base was something she actively avoided. She recognised at work, for example, that she was more comfortable in an unsupportive environment. She could exercise her self-reliance to the full. She also recognised the dangers inherent within this. When she moved to a more supportive environment, she was made uneasy by the secure base her manager and the team provided. As we explored this together, she experimented with accepting and using this security.

Within her relationship with Andrew an opposite tendency was emerging. She welcomed Andrew as a secure base, becoming very needy of his availability and anxious when away from him. She recognised in this a fear that eventually she would wear him out. As with many of the children I have worked with, the move away from avoidant attachment relationships leads initially to ambivalent attachment behaviours. Alexia was testing out needing someone; she was responding to someone wanting to care for her, but this battled with a fear that she would eventually lose this relationship too. She was not yet secure within her relationship with Andrew. She needed to ensure he stayed available by expressing a high level of attachment need. She needed to test his constancy by pushing him away. The push and pull demonstrated her developing ambivalence: 'I want to need but I fear it too. I pull you towards me, but when it gets too scary, I push you away. I need to check you will stay.' She needed Andrew to hold steady through her ambivalence so that security could grow.

These two experiences, at work and home, provided Alexia with a juxtaposition within which she was learning healthy dependence and independence. Finding this balance in her relationship with me helped her to explore this within the relationships that surrounded her. This exploration allowed Alexia to discover ways to find more nuanced positions between the extremes she often held. Alexia saw the world in black and white but was discovering a world in colour. She was learning that she needed both roots and wings.

Alexia's attitude to the Russian Doll parts of herself was another example of seeking this balancing point. Her tendency towards seeing things as black and white led her to dichotomise her experience as false (bad) and real (good). I used Stephen Porges' idea of defences as heroic to help her to relax this dichotomy (Porges 2017). Defences develop for a good reason and are needed at the time. Defences can literally be life-saving. They can continue to be useful at times. We explored together ways that Alexia could embrace her defences. She did not want to be driven by them any more, but she could take back the driving seat and discover how to use them flexibly. As Alexia relaxed her rigidity, she was able to respond more flexibly to a range of experiences, choosing how to manage these experiences. She was learning how to use roots, and this in turn helped her to develop a healthy independence, caring for others and seeking help for herself as needed. Her wings were more robust because of the roots she was finding.

At times within our sessions, younger parts of Alexia would emerge as we worked on finding balance within her life. These parts were most evident in her relationship to me as a mother figure. Alexia saw in me a potential mother, in place of her birth mother who had not been able to meet her need for an unconditional relationship. I offered an unconditional acceptance as therapist. I could not meet all the unfulfilled need from her infancy. I could therefore be a 'mother figure' in my acceptance, support and guidance. I could not be her mother. The mature Alexia understood this, whilst the younger Alexia felt anger at any sign that someone or something else was more important than her to me. Even something as simple as looking out of the window, or checking the time, made her annoyed; it was evidence that she wasn't the centre of my world. Alexia was an infant who needed me to be totally absorbed with her. She was also an adult, with an adult understanding of the relationship that I offered.

This could be unbalancing for me. I needed to offer a stable relationship across her ages. Alexia reflected that she was doing nearly three decades of development all at once, and it could be unnerving for both of us. Gradually, however, these different parts became an integrated part of herself. She grieved for the mother I could not be whilst using the therapist relationship I provided, and, in the process, the younger parts of herself became absorbed into her sense of herself as a whole. Alexia could recognise elements of them within her day-to-day functioning. She noticed, for example, being able to express the sense of fun of a toddler or the anxiety of an adolescent whilst maintaining her sense of self as a whole, independent adult.

Chapter 6

MOVING TOWARDS ACCEPTANCE AND FINDING WOBBLY GROUND

FINDING ME

I want to feel complete. Not painted but real, the authentic me comfortable with contradictions; embracing all the dolls that have been and are part of me. I learn that 'it is as it is'. The sum of the parts is a whole. Only in wholeness will I be healthy and complete, both vulnerable and invulnerable, dependent and independent, able to help and be helped, caring and cared for.

This still frightens me. I cannot yet accept the baby me – too scary to be so vulnerable and needy. I hate and fear this part of me. I want it to go away. I need time; not yet, but soon. I cannot yet believe that it is okay to have needs of my own.

The angry part is a little easier. I learn the strength it has given me. I am still frightened of it overwhelming me, but I learn to accept these feelings. I grow stronger, more able to regulate the strong feelings – assertive, not angry. Sometimes it overwhelms me still. I have to be kind to myself, forgiving. Forgiveness is hard, it embraces difference, black and white feels easier but harsher. I am learning to live with conflicting feelings, but it is hard. I can be good and bad. That is okay!

I also need to understand this in others. Father is easier, but it is contradictory. He is good and caring, and yet he abandoned me. How can I reconcile these? I want it to be black and white. I am learning to accept that life isn't that simple. I can enjoy my developing relationship with him. Mother is harder, I can't reconcile my feelings towards her.

I hate the golden child. She feels the most dishonest part of me. I am angry that she fooled so many, and yet I worked so hard to do so. I am reminded that this is control of a different kind, but still a heroic defence. If only I hadn't needed her deception for so long. Approval for this child was always conditional. If only others could have seen within and unconditionally loved the whole of me.

I am done meeting others' needs without reciprocation. I am sad as I fear this will mean losing them. Do I have to lose them to find me?

I know I cannot meet all the needs others put on me. I start to put in boundaries. In trying to meet all their needs whilst sacrificing mine, I wasn't helping anyone. I learn I can help them better from a distance. I can't do it all, but I will do what I can to the best of my ability.

I see it is difficult for others to witness this change in me. I have to be strong as I am pulled back into old ways, old patterns. I hold on to the belief that it is better for all of us this way. I feel guilty that I am getting the help that I also want for them. I wish that we could do this journey together, but I know each of us must find our own path.

I feel the ground getting wobbly beneath me. I am anxious.

It feels uncomfortable. You tell me this is healthy, that only in shaking everything up will I find the authentic me.

I learn to be brave, to live with the anxiety, but it is exhausting. I sleep a lot. I don't know who I am any more, but I know I want to be more than the parts of myself. I can't live fragmented, but I do not yet feel whole. I keep a foot in the old world as I put a foot into the new. The new world feels unsteady, I am pulled back into the old. I feel the oscillations as I try out new ways of being with others and then retreat into old familiar patterns. I find it hard to believe that I can have relationships built on reciprocity and not through pleasing them, giving them what they want. You help me to believe that I can find equal relationships and the confidence to know that I am wanted for myself.

I am me. I am vulnerable, needy, angry and pleasing. And I am so much more. As I accept most of the parts of me, I start to become whole, integrated.

I still have self-doubt. The old patterns are there to seduce me still. This too is a part of who I am. I love the Russian Doll with all the parts. They saved me. They are part of me, but I am not painted any more. I am real. I am authentic. I am me.

There is trauma also. I hear things that are not happening. It is confusing. I am surprised that I carry trauma that I can't see. I hear high-pitched angry voices and they frighten me. I am not sure who they belong to. I hear a voice shouting that she wants to get rid of me. Is it you, Mother? Did you say this to me? It is what I feel but is it true? Or does the angry voice belong to him? Is this why I was so frightened? Is this why I had to be so good? How many angry voices were there?

Through all this work my siblings are there needing me. I worry for them, but I cannot be who they want me to be. I am angry with Mother for abandoning us all.

Reflections from Alexia

What I was discovering in therapy had parallels in my present life. Previously I had always relied on others' opinions of me. These guided me. How I viewed myself, how I acted, how I was, were all based on what others wanted. In therapy I was starting to look at this differently. This gave me confidence to make changes in my life. I was learning to be confident that I knew what was best for me. I was learning the difference between being independent, relying on no-one but myself, and learning to seek support, asking for help when needed. This wasn't without its challenges. It felt like I was taking huge risks. I worried that my need would be insatiable and wear others out. I might be left worse off and alone. After each risk, when I attempted to seek support, I would retreat a little. I could only do this one step at a time.

I was being challenged to own parts of me that I found difficult to accept. Parts that had been hidden in order to please others. This was really difficult in terms of acceptance. I was learning to accept that it was okay to trust myself, and that meant all parts of myself, even those parts that I wanted to banish. On the one hand this felt really genuine, authentic. But on the other hand, I still feared those parts would be unacceptable to others. A part of me was still driven to seek approval. I was, however, slowly moving towards figuring out that the only person's approval I needed was my own.

This was ridiculously unsettling and new. Prior to this I had no idea that this was even a way of being; it felt utterly alien. I had spent my whole life learning to be what others wanted me to be. I came into therapy believing that Kim was going to teach me how to be even better at doing this, and it was a shock to discover that she wasn't going to do this. I had no idea what self-acceptance was, never mind how to recognise my own needs.

I realised that this was being mirrored in most of the relationships around me. I figured out what they wanted from me and then tried to give them this. Anything else I would hide away. Growing up, no-one modelled to me any other way. I had no template for how to be different. There was no-one to show me an authentic way of being.

Within therapy, Kim was constantly modelling acceptance. She showed me over and over again that I was acceptable to her. Whenever we discovered the 'unacceptable' parts of me I would think this is it; this time she will know just how bad I really am. This was hidden for a reason, and uncovering it felt a huge risk. But every time there was an opportunity to find me unacceptable, Kim just came back with acceptance. This felt intolerable for a while. I couldn't understand it. I was just waiting for the thing that would find me out. I was certain that the next thing would be it. When it wasn't, I would find a story to explain why; it was her job, she wasn't understanding what I was really like, she was just being kind. I could not accept her acceptance.

I found ways to test Kim's commitment to me. It felt too good to be true. I did not feel I could be acceptable to anyone and I had to find out the limit here. Waiting to be found out was unbearable. I would disclose things about myself just to bring it on; waiting was too hard.

This came to a head when Kim left me alone for a while to deal with an incident outside of the room. We could hear shouting, and as she left the room, I just knew it was about me. I heard things being smashed and someone screaming, 'Get rid of her.' Although I had known that this would happen, that one day Kim would leave me, in that moment I was caught off guard. I had relaxed and now felt ambushed. In that moment I felt totally unacceptable and knew I was going to be banished. I started to tell myself I needed to leave. I just wanted to flee. I had no words to explain this, I just knew we were done and wanted to get out. I felt as if I was in a black hole. I was totally focused on the words I was hearing and the panic I was experiencing at being found out.

When Kim came back, she spent a long time helping me to

calm down. I needed this time. At first, she tried to help me feel better too quickly. This made me angry with her. In the moment it felt like so many other relationships in my past. I was being told to get over it. When Kim moved back to acceptance, I felt relief. She recognised that she was getting it wrong, and took the time to make it right again. Now I could calm and could start to think again.

I began to realise that what I had been hearing hadn't actually happened. Someone was shouting but this wasn't about me and no ornaments were being smashed. We figured out that I was hearing voices from my past. Now I felt completely confused as I began to realise that what I had experienced hadn't actually happened. Somehow present and past had got mixed up.

This whole experience was pivotal for me. I think that this was the first time I truly believed that Kim did find me acceptable. Even when I was angry with her, this did not falter. I felt that she had seen the worst of me and still hadn't sent me away. I had always experienced myself as unacceptable to my mother; she did not love me and wanted me gone as an infant. This had developed into a belief that I was unlovable and unacceptable, and only if I hid myself and my feelings would others accept me. Anger was the most dangerous feeling to reveal, it would lead to instant abandonment. Kim's acceptance of my anger, therefore, was a massive contradiction to this belief. I could not hold on to my experience of Kim's acceptance and my belief in my own unacceptability. Something had to shift.

Finally, I could believe in Kim's acceptance. It had taken a long time, but I got it. I was ready to explore holding acceptance for myself. Reflecting on this now is hard. This was a really emotional experience. Despite how hard it was, I can see how important it was that this happened. We needed this break and repair for me to see that even at the worst of times it would be okay.

Looking back, this marked a turning point in therapy. It felt like there was another way, another path was being formed. This was scary. A new path meant change and risk. It also felt really hopeful. Different paths mean choices about which one to follow. This was the first time in my life I had a choice about how to be. You don't have to be defined by the path that was given to you. There is a different way.

Hopeful and scary. Things that are familiar feel safe and this is comforting. I knew what the risks were. I had learned how to deal with them. There is a lot of unknown in following the new path. How could I trust that the risks that came with the new path would not be as bad as or even worse than the risks of remaining on the old path? I remember feeling like I had a foot in each camp. I was trying to walk on both paths at the same time. Parts of me still walked on the old path whilst the new emerging parts of me encouraged me along a new path.

I was beginning to want to fight for what I needed. This is what Angry Doll had given me. I was angry with others for not recognising these needs. I wasn't going to let them be missed any more. This also gave me a drive to find a different way of understanding why my needs hadn't been met. The way I had understood it, that my needs weren't important, was not making sense any more.

I loved my newly found assertiveness. I found a fire within me. A fire that had been doused so long ago. Once I found this, I wasn't going to let it go again. This is the first part of me that felt authentic. This is the first time that I liked something about myself. I was indignant that I had to deny this part of myself in order to survive. Anger, indignation, and under this a well of grief that I hadn't been taken care of as a baby.

Reflections from Kim

Within the DDP model we often remind ourselves to 'trust the process'. It is easy to feel a pressure to do something; to find the golden elixir disguised as 'therapy' that others expect us to have.

This is a false expectation; it assumes that the therapist has a way of 'fixing' the client, much as a physician diagnoses a problem and finds a treatment. Belief in a fix often comes with assumptions about a time frame. Find the problem, apply the fix and discharge. The patient is passive, and the physician is expert. Whilst this can work in physical medicine, it is rarely a helpful model for psychological interventions.

The pressure to fix can push the therapist into taking a more expert role: I know best, so do as I say. This can move us into lecturing or problem-solving with our clients. This meets a need in ourselves, in response to the expectations of others. Neither lecturing nor problem-solving is wrong; it is about the timing and purpose of these. Lectures in the form of psychoeducation can be helpful, and Alexia and I with our mutual interest in psychology would spend times in the sessions thinking about her experiences from a psychological and neurobiological viewpoint, understanding what might be going on within her brain and nervous system. Similarly, there were times when it was helpful to focus on a problem and find answers to it. Thus, we might explore times when she felt triggered by her past experience increasing her anxiety in the present. We discussed different strategies she could try to help her to regulate her anxiety at these times. We combined our expertise and, in the process, discovered what was useful to Alexia.

DDP is collaborative. Alexia and I worked together. Alexia needed to guide me as much as I was guiding her. Even when it was unconscious, she would let me know what she needed next. She would point the way whilst I helped her to go further than she could alone. In this way we discovered together who she was, how she became that person and who she could be. This was the process. Together we could help the process to work. This work was intense and highly emotional. The move into more reflective and less affective modes of being, as in psychoeducation and problem-solving, provided natural breaks from this intensity. Often, we would do this towards the end of the session. This allowed Alexia to move out of affective as she prepared to re-enter the outside world. I was acutely aware that Alexia had to drive home after our sessions and that she would be carrying a lot of emotion within her still. Helping her to move into reflective, I hoped, would also help her to manage this safely.

When working with children I would often notice that following more emotionally intense sessions they needed something lighter. They would decline my invitations to move into more emotional depth in the following session. I anticipated that Alexia might need the same and would at times plan to keep a session lighter and more reflective. This invariably failed. Alexia often worked at a faster pace than I was expecting, and would quickly lead me into the emotional work of therapy. I learnt to hold lightly to any agenda or plan I held for the session. Following Alexia's lead took us into deeper exploration very naturally. Follow-lead-follow was an important principle to guide my work with Alexia and ensured I didn't try to steer her away from where she needed to be.

The metaphor of a journey is an obvious one for the process of therapy, but this is how it felt. I accompanied Alexia upon a journey of self-discovery. I could only go at her pace. At each stage I needed to listen to Alexia; to interpret where she needed to go next. I could not push her faster than she could manage. She did not let me go slower than she needed.

There was no resistance to the therapy. We did, however, need to work with resistance to acceptance. Alexia wanted the difficult stuff to disappear; I gently challenged her to accept the difficult stuff, using my empathy and compassion to help her to develop the same.

This acceptance meant that Alexia was becoming more aware of the effects of trauma. At times she doubted that she was traumatised. This fitted her narrative that she was making a mountain out of a molehill, that others had experienced far worse. As the impact of trauma became more apparent, it was harder to maintain this. Alexia became more aware of trauma being triggered within her: she noticed themes in dreams and nightmares, recollections could be intrusive as memories came to her unbidden, making it hard to focus on what she was doing. Very occasionally she would experience a flashback memory: an experience of being back at the time the trauma was happening. As therapist it can be hard to witness this. It can appear that progress is moving backwards as trauma symptoms become more apparent. It was important for me to remember that in her avoidance, trauma had not gone away, just underground. As Alexia allowed herself to experience them now, she was also learning to manage the impact of trauma. This was progress.

Much of the time this happened outside of the therapy room, as triggers within her world arose. On one occasion Alexia experienced a flashback during therapy whilst I was out of the room. I came back to find Alexia curled into a foetal position in the chair. She had heard breakages and anger, triggered by someone shouting in another room. She was back in a childhood experience of being shouted at. She heard high-pitched, angry voices telling her that they wanted to get rid of her. She appeared very young in both voice and mannerisms as she moved into the shame that had been ever-present at the time of the memory. This shame became confused with her relationship with me, and this confusion was increased because I had been out of the room. She wanted to leave immediately. She felt she was undeserving of my attention, that others needed me. I should get rid of her.

I felt that it was important that she stay. I wanted Alexia to experience co-regulation, allowing her to move out of the panic that was overtaking her. I was also aware that I was feeling guilty that I had left her alone, and urgently wanted to repair any relationship rupture that had occurred. In my anxiety I became less open to Alexia and more defensive. This was clear as I rushed to reassure her rather than staying with co-regulation. I tried to convince Alexia of things she could not feel; that I did not want to get rid of her. She needed my empathy for how hard it was to experience me as being there for her when she was feeling so undeserving. Reassurance jumped over the empathy. In trying to convince her, my unconditional acceptance had slipped. Alexia was feeling angry with me. My clumsiness in trying to repair one rupture had led to another rupture between us.

Gradually we both calmed down and I became open and engaged again to what Alexia needed. Empathy reasserted itself. Alexia was able to regulate and emerge out of this trauma response. Now we could reflect. We talked over what had happened and she was shocked to discover that what she had heard had not occurred. I noticed with her how flashback memories worked and how dysregulating this can be. We thought about what had helped her to calm, my role in this and the mistakes I had made. We explored her feelings of anger towards me and my acceptance of this. We explored the importance of repairing ruptures and the value this placed on the relationship. At the time I felt I had let Alexia down. Over time it became an important experience of how things could go wrong and be put right. I had fallen from a pedestal of perfect therapist, and this was a good fall. Alexia was learning about human relationships. She was better able to appreciate my unconditional acceptance through witnessing the importance I put in the relationship and repairing ruptures when they inevitably occur. She was learning a new way of being, an imperfect self in imperfect relationships. A way of being she had not experienced in her own childhood.

Witnessing Alexia's gradually developing acceptance was one of the most satisfying parts of the work for me. To do this though, I had to accompany her onto the wobbly ground that lies between defence and authenticity.

The most uncomfortable part of therapy for both client and therapist is the removal of the solid ground that the client has been living on, whilst not yet having new ground to replace it with. This is a time both for moving forward and for retreating, as therapist and client build the new ground together. This was both an uncomfortable and an exciting time for Alexia. The possibility of finding new ways of being kept her going.

Developmentally, this phase felt like Alexia moving into adolescence. Teenagers move out and back to family as they explore a growing independence. They often wobble and family is there to support them. When Alexia wobbled therapy was her support. She would talk with me about her attempts at being more authentic with work, family and friends. We would discuss times when her old anxieties and fears re-emerged, and her ambivalence became more apparent.

As therapist I experienced myself as a bridge that could help Alexia to make this journey. Holding this bridge steady helped to reduce the wobbliness she was experiencing. This did mean I needed to be careful not to wobble myself. Retreating to the familiar was a danger we both experienced.

I remember as a new therapist noticing that I could influence my clients to move towards or away from experience. I would notice their increasing affect and gently move them back into, what felt to me, the safer territory of thinking. Cognitive behaviour therapy (CBT) was a model that provided me with tools to do this.

As I studied DDP I came to realise how unhelpful this could be. CBT was a way for me to hold on to my own defences, allowing them to influence the therapeutic process. In effect, I was using the model to strengthen the habit of thinking over feeling, not opening the way for integration of emotional experience. This is not to suggest that CBT is an unhelpful intervention, but more that I could use it unhelpfully because of my own level of discomfort with emotional experience. When working with Alexia I needed to be aware of this, ensuring that I was focused on what she needed despite how uncomfortable this might make us in the moment. I needed to find a balance between reflecting and experiencing that was right for Alexia. In this way the bridge I was providing could take her across the wobbly ground towards a new way of being, integrated and whole.

The old ground, although unhealthy, is comfortable because it is familiar. Alexia wobbled as she moved away from this. We saw this as a sign of health and recovery. Much anxiety accompanied the journey from the old to the new. There was no other way around. Not being able to tolerate this anxiety can mean the client becomes stuck on the old ground. Whilst we were building a relationship, exploring Alexia's story and working out how she could take care of herself better, she was building this tolerance. She was ready to move on through the wobbly ground, trusting that firm ground lay ahead.

As we progressed with this work, I noticed that Alexia was integrating her anger. She did not need to hide it in Angry Doll any more. This allowed her to feel proud of the assertive parts of herself. As she described experiences she was having between sessions, I could see a more confidently assertive person emerging. This, coupled with the compassion towards herself that she was developing, allowed her to find more balance in her personal and work relationships.

In this way we continued to work with the range of emotional experience that Alexia found within her. Alexia was learning to manage emotions that she had previously made go away. This was the new ground that she was moving on to and it was exhausting.

Chapter 7

FINDING THE BABY AND LOSING MOTHER

FINDING ME

I know there is still work to do. I am still angry with the baby doll. I want to tell her to stop being so needy. She carries all the 'bad' that I have run from all my life. I want her to stay hidden. I fear what others will see if she becomes part of me. Can I be truly authentic without her? Can others live with me if she is seen? My mother told me I was bad. Have I taken over from her in keeping this part of me hidden?

Even whilst I resist, I feel this part of myself. I feel little. I feel needy. I am jealous when others get attention from her. I want it all.

I feel the badness in me rising up. I fear you will see it. I fear losing all those who love me when they know what lies within. I am so angry with the baby me. She is the demon within. She needed so much. She raged. She was powerful. She could kill. Is this where the badness began? But she was scared. How would she survive? I cry, I am sad, but all I feel is anger. Why did you have to be so needy?

And then it changes. I allow the sadness in. I see the baby for who she is, tiny, vulnerable, immature. She should have been taken care of. I am angry with Mother. The baby appeared well cared for, but she was left all alone. It was unfair. I feel pain for this smallest part of me. She had no-one to care for her.

Why am I so upset? I want this to be gone. I don't want to feel this pain and sadness. And yet it is part of me. I fear for the baby, but I am strong. I can grow.

I am a baby who grows into a child. A child who pleases. A child who learns to smile. Check in the mirror. Is the smile in place? Notice how the smile does not reach my eyes. No-one sees. The baby is lost.

I accept the baby part of myself. This comes with a cost. I am deeply sad. I will care for the baby, but it feels like giving up on Mother. She will never be there. She will never be the mother I long for.

I feel stronger. I am well. I have fewer headaches. I have done nearly three decades of development in a few months. I have learnt to be dependent whilst also learning independence. I feel different, both more vulnerable and stronger. It is no longer black and white. I see in colour!

I revisit feelings for Mother. I am so angry. I am so sad. Longing and grief fill me up. My grief is all-consuming. Without you I would be lost in it. You help me to be strong enough to embrace the feelings I have hidden from all my life. It makes me sad. It makes me brave. I find the strength to acknowledge my need.

She was so confusing, both nice and cruel. Always unpredictable. Will you be cross? No, you are laughing. It is okay. But now you are cross. You tell me you are angry with me. I feel unloved. I am locked in. I want my auntie. You tell me I am naughty. I have to stay locked in.

Now Mother is poorly. I look after the children. Mother lies down. I am so scared. She disappears for weeks, and then she is back. It is fun again. It is confusing.

I want to tell you how angry I am. The adult me knows you couldn't help it. I feel sorry for you. The child does not want to feel sorry. I want you to know what you have done. I am so sad that you cannot feel remorse for how you treated me. I grieve for the mother I will never find.

My anger reduces, it is spent. I feel sympathy for you. I will always regret but I know the problems you faced. The grief is easier to live with now. I hope your story will not be mine. Will this work help me to avoid your fate?

Now I have space to think about Father. He is here. He regrets. Can I forgive him for leaving us in foster care? For finding a new life without us? He is back now, trying to make amends. Sometimes I punish him for not being perfect. Sometimes I feel not good enough for him. We both make mistakes.

What is unconditional love? I seek perfect relationships. I learn that good enough can be good enough. We are imperfect. Relationships rupture and then they repair. This is unconditional. I sought perfection; the perfect, unconditional relationship. I discovered something else. Unconditional does not mean never making mistakes. Unconditional means the relationship is important enough to seek repair. The world has just turned 360 degrees.

Reflections from Alexia

I had to embrace Baby Doll. I had known this for a while but had resisted for so long. This was a piece of the work I didn't want to do; I was absolutely terrified. During these sessions I would find things to talk about with Kim, current events in my life that would interest her. Anything to delay the moment when we would move on to what I knew was inevitable. I would have talked for the whole time, whilst Kim gently encouraged me to face what I feared. It was only my trust in her that carried me forward.

Up until now we had what I saw as a nice accepting narrative of how I had come to be who I was. This was the 'what if' moment. What if this narrative is all wrong and I really am all bad? Maybe that is why everything happened to me. The baby doll could be my undoing. It seemed ironic that we hadn't even realised that there was a baby doll hidden within the Russian Doll. This part was hidden in many ways. I was so annoyed when Kim unstuck the doll and the baby emerged. Now we had to explore it!

Kim switched to an actual toy baby doll at this point. This was a really hard part of the therapy. I was confronting how I felt about this part of myself. I was taking some big risks in exposing this. Always the ever-present danger that Kim would agree with the view of myself that I held. When she didn't, I had to confront a different possibility. The way I saw the most vulnerable parts of myself did not have to be the literal truth.

This went hand in hand with my experience of a baby of a close friend. I remember watching as everyone delighted in him and he naturally became the centre of everyone's universe. I was part of this, I loved and adored him too. This also brought up intense sadness that I hadn't had this myself. I finally saw that no baby could be responsible for not being taken care of. That was not a decision that they could hold. I could find nothing about this baby boy not to love, so what was it about me that was so unlovable?

I remember Kim presenting the idea that maybe this was how Mum felt too. Maybe this is what I saw in her eyes when I looked at her. Maybe this is why I had always believed this about myself. I had an external narrative of what Mum had shown me. I wasn't born like this. This had been projected into me.

I could see my friend's baby developing within the relationships around him, and realised that this had also happened to me, but in a totally different way. This baby learned he was lovable, I learned I wasn't. I could now hold a different truth. Mum showed me I was unlovable. With Kim, with Andrew, and finally for myself, I was beginning to discover something different. The odds were stacking up, not everybody could be wrong. Maybe I was lovable after all.

By accepting that I had been an innocent infant with my own needs, I also had to accept that Mum couldn't meet these. It was at this time that I realised that it wasn't any unconditional mother that I wanted, I wanted my own mother. I wanted her to unconditionally love me. In accepting that it was not my fault that I had felt unlovable, I also had to accept that I could not make that better. No matter how 'good' I became, I could not make her what I needed her to be. This wasn't in my control. All the controlling behaviours I had found were now to no avail. This turned my world upside down.

I needed to grieve the loss of the mother I had always believed could be there for me if only I could make myself good enough. I also needed to face the reality that all of the women I had sought as mother could also never truly be my mum. I needed something from my birth mother that no-one else could give me. The loss of this was hard, especially with Kim and my foster mother. Any fantasy that they would turn into my mum was gone. I was grieving for my mum and for my hope of all the other potential mums.

There was something I had recognised in Kim when I first met her all those years before that had led me to contact her. It was ironic that Kim reminded me of my mum in some of her features. I thought of her as like my mum but a nicer version. Whilst we both felt the pull to be mother and daughter, we both also maintained a boundary around this that kept our therapy relationship healthy. The adult me knew that this was the right thing to do and Kim was aware of the boundaries we needed to maintain; boundaries which I knew we needed even whilst I mourned what could not be.

These revelations opened the door to my grief. I was letting nearly three decades' worth of grief out. It was totally over-whelming. It spilled over into all parts of my life. Any image or representation of mothers, a film, a song, seeing a mother in a shop, seeing someone pregnant, would knock me sideways. I needed to grieve my birth mother before I could let any other mother figures in my life help me. Only by accepting this grief could I turn to others for support, without the need to control that had been my constant companion.

This piece of work also helped me to find my true place in my foster family: neither birth daughter nor outsider, an accepted part of the family. It led me to realise that no-one could replace my mum, and in accepting this I could claim my foster mother. I no longer had to put her on a pedestal that she could never achieve. I had been completely reliant on my foster mother's opinions. I had tried to gauge this so I could be what she wanted, an attempt to find the 'mother' I longed for. It was in vain; the mother I wanted was my birth mother. She could never be that no matter how hard I worked to please her. Now I did not need her approval of me any more. I no longer needed to control my relationship with her. This paved the way for us finding an authentic relationship together.

We also explored my relationship with my dad and my auntie. This felt more complicated than with my mother, as it did later when we explored my uncle. I knew I had unresolved feelings about them, and with Kim's encouragement and support I could express my feelings of anger towards them. With Dad and my aunt this felt harder. I did feel angry, but also, I had memories of a loving relationship. I had experienced a positive relationship with them, tinged with the negative elements – my dad had left us and neither of them had protected me from the abuse I was experiencing. I also felt Kim's empathy for them, and I wanted to find this empathy too. This made it harder to express anger towards them. Maybe this made it more difficult to access the negative feelings. It wasn't black and white, and I struggled with the in between.

I think we gave a lot of time (which was needed) to processing my anger with Mum. Upon reflection I'd have liked to have done some empty chair work around my feelings for my aunt and dad too. I think in my black and white way of being, it was more straightforward to be angry with Mum and not angry with Dad and my aunt. I very much put them on a pedestal of being perfect when I was younger. This is the way I've approached it since I was tiny, so that it wasn't all of the adults in my life who caused me pain. As I became more flexible, I could see that I was rightly angry towards Dad and my aunt as well. This feels healthier and more balanced.

With all these relationships, grief is still there; I guess it will never leave. It is more acceptable to me now. In accepting this it has freed up other relationships.

Reflections from Kim

Within therapy, Alexia was learning that she could be vulnerable and let others support her. Alexia anticipated that vulnerability would weaken her. Instead she was discovering that it made her stronger.

Our sessions continued with the same rhythm; we began with a catch-up and then the theme for the session would emerge. This might come out of a reflection from Alexia about her current experience, it might come from a dream or memory she had, or it might arise out of a question I asked. I would notice a change in Alexia as I gently pursued the theme. It is hard to explain but she would look younger and more vulnerable. Sometimes she would cry, but almost seemed unaware of her tears until I passed her a tissue. At other times she would talk with surprise at how easily the tears came from just a simple thought or reflection. We would then work with what was emerging until it was time to lighten again. Alexia would sit up straighter and we would chat until it was time to end; processing what we had been experiencing within the session. This pattern was a constant to our sessions; over time it became easier for Alexia to manage the transitions within this pattern. I also noticed that leaving was becoming easier for her. She was more trusting that I would be constant. Leaving is much easier when you are confident you will return.

We continued to work backwards through the layers represented by the Russian Doll. We were getting closer to the innermost doll and one of the biggest challenges. Alexia wanted to ignore this part for a long time. Finding the smallest baby doll within our Russian Doll led to a shift. Alexia was ready to explore this part of herself. Alexia had strong feelings about this baby part of herself. We needed to explore these. In order to do this, we moved away from the Russian Doll, using a toy baby doll instead. The baby doll looked more vulnerable and infant-like. Working with this doll therefore helped us to access the feelings evoked within Alexia.

Alexia was initially angry with the doll, perceiving it as a demon that had led to all her problems. She was disgusted by its vulnerability and neediness. She could barely look at the doll and she could not pick it up. I was struck by how powerful a symbol the doll was. It helped us understand Alexia's experience much more quickly and deeply than if we had just talked together about it. The doll also helped Alexia to interact with this experience. This allowed Alexia to move into her feelings in a very real and vivid way. At my suggestion Alexia talked to the doll. Still she would not look at it as she told it of all she felt. Her feelings of self-hatred, shame and blame were spoken to the doll very directly. Alexia was exploring how she felt about herself. She was also learning why she felt this way. Together we recognised how dangerous her vulnerability had felt when she was little. The doll helped us to experience the fear a child can have when her needs are not being met. The terror, the isolation and the confusion were all there. The doll took us back to an infancy that Alexia recognised as her own. It also allowed us to know the longing she had for it to be different. A longing wrapped up in her own unworthiness. If she hadn't been needy, small and weak, she would have been lovable. Accepting this 'truth' of Alexia's opened a pathway to explore alternative 'truths' in time.

Never was 'trust the process' more needed by me than during this part of the work. I longed to pick up the doll and cradle it; to confront Alexia with its immaturity. How could it have been responsible for what she had experienced from her mother? I wanted to make Alexia see the doll for what it represented, an innocent baby. Instead, I worked hard to stay with acceptance of the emotion that Alexia was expressing, reminding myself of what I frequently tell others: that this emotion is neither right nor wrong, it just is.

Of course, over the sessions, Alexia's feelings towards the doll did change. It was a very emotional moment, the day she leaned forward and picked up the doll. She cradled it to her, embracing it, accepting its vulnerability and lack of culpability. This felt like a significant step forward. The ground beneath her was less wobbly as she discovered this renewed part of herself. Alexia was journeying into a new world, one where she noticed how differently she was experiencing herself.

Bringing a doll into the work led to a responsibility on my part: how to care for the doll. It had become a powerful symbol of our work with the baby part of Alexia. In between sessions I needed to put it somewhere that felt right for both of us. We chose to wrap it in a blanket and leave it in the therapy room. Somehow the sight of this doll, nurtured by the blanket but utterly alone, resonated strongly with my experience of Alexia's story. To the outside world she appeared cared for, but she experienced her mother as emotionally unavailable. At the end of this part of the work we discussed what would now happen to the doll. We wondered whether Alexia should take it home with her, but this did not feel right. This part of the work was finished. The doll became just a doll again, going back into my therapy cupboard.

Alexia was learning to accept the different parts of herself, embracing the emotions that she had hidden within these parts. She was learning to feel comfortable with being vulnerable, having needs, letting others help and care for her. In doing this she was also opening herself up to more pain. When you no longer blame yourself, who can you blame? Alexia was confronting what she had always wanted: a mother she longed for but never had. It was tempting to move from blaming herself to blaming her mother. This was not our journey, however. I supported Alexia to take the more complicated route towards understanding. Blame was a short cut that led to a dead end. We were not able to understand Alexia's birth mother, this was a story that was not ours to explore. We could, however, have some glimpses of this through the impact upon Alexia. Our goal was to understand this impact. Through this understanding lay the empathy and compassion that Alexia needed to find for herself. Understanding was a double-edged sword, however. Understanding also opened up a world of loss and longing. Alexia moved into an intense period of grieving the lack of an unconditional mother in her life.

As we worked with the parts of the Russian Doll, and then with Baby Doll, we were taken into an exploration of the different mother figures that Alexia had experienced. This included her birth mother and two foster mothers. Alexia recognised some conditionality in all these relationships.

The most significant maternal loss for Alexia was of course her birth mother. Working with this was therefore the most intense emotionally. I have tried to capture something of the experience of this work, and Alexia's relationship with her birth mother, in the story at the end of this chapter.

As when exploring Baby Doll, I felt that we needed an object, a symbol to represent this mother. Something that we could work with to help Alexia fully experience the depth of what she felt. Something to allow her to express the kaleidoscope of feelings this aroused. I thought of doing this psychodramatically, using spontaneous dramatization via role play, to move into and out of the role of mother. I had seen this done before very effectively. I was not confident, however. I doubted my acting skills and was also uneasy about moving into and out of a role when I also needed to stay present for Alexia, helping her to absorb and contain the emotion she would be experiencing. There was no other attachment figure present to do this. I therefore chose to use an empty chair. In the room was a wicker chair that we had not used to sit on. I could easily move this forward and backwards as needed. When I brought it before us it would become a representation of the person as experienced by Alexia. When I moved it back it became an unused chair again.

The chair as 'mother' allowed Alexia to express the feelings she carried in relation to her mother. This work was inspired by Gestalt therapy, allowing Alexia to gain insight into her feelings about the interpersonal relationships she had encountered in her past (Perls 1992). DDP provided me with ways of adapting this technique. I did not ask Alexia to sit in the chair to talk for the other. I worried that this would be too frightening an experience; it would bring her too closely in touch with those who had abused or neglected her. Instead we left the chair empty and I would use 'talking for and about' as ways of helping the dialogue to develop.

The empty chair allowed Alexia to explore her experience of her mother and to express the range of feelings she had, including the now familiar mix of anger, pain and sadness. I could help her with this, encouraging her to find the words she wanted to say, and stepping in to find them for her when this was too difficult. 'Talking for' was a powerful use of the DDP principles to help me to find words for Alexia when she struggled. I would talk as if I was Alexia, checking with her that I was getting the words right, or whether I had missed anything in what I was saying on her behalf.

The co-creation of story that we had previously engaged in helped me to find the right words. Experiencing Alexia's response to these words, both verbal and non-verbal, helped me to give her words that were hers. I had to ensure that I did not put into words what I wanted Alexia to express rather than what she needed to express. Our intersubjective connection guided me so that I could avoid this mistake. If I did say the wrong thing or express something the wrong way, Alexia guided me back. I did not have to worry about getting this right. As long as I stayed attuned to Alexia, I would find my way, even if I stumbled sometimes.

I also 'talked for' her birth mother, discovering that it was harder to find the right words when doing this. Should I be challenging, or contrite? Did Alexia need to hear 'Mother' justifying her deeds so that she could respond to this or did she need some resolution through hearing regret and remorse? I needed to be confident trying out different voices, again trusting in my relationship with Alexia to guide me to what was helpful and to move away from what was not. In this way I discovered that it was not helpful to express remorse. Alexia experienced this as unreal and minimising of her experience. She had sadness that her mother had never been able to understand why her children had been removed. Giving a voice to remorse therefore felt wrong, a microrupture in my attunement with Alexia. Her trust meant that she could put me right, the rupture was repaired, and I understood better what I needed to do. Alexia needed to sit with the sadness of a mother who she did not experience as remorseful. It was important that I didn't try to make this sadness go away through the experiential work.

Letting Alexia leave after these sessions was especially hard. I knew that Alexia would be carrying a lot of feelings with her as she left. I needed to trust in her ability to take care of herself, resisting an impulse to check in with her.

Alexia had many dreams about her mother during this part of the work. This was not unexpected. We would discuss these in the sessions, exploring the meanings embedded in the dreams, deepening our understanding of Alexia's experience. Mixed in with these was a recurring dream about a tiger, preying upon her. We puzzled about this. It felt sinister, and we wondered what experience of her mother had led to this feeling of danger represented by the tiger. This dream was also foreshadowing work that we needed to do later, although we didn't understand this at the time. We thought that the tiger represented her mother, and we still think it does. Later we understood that there was also a very different significance represented by the symbol of a tiger.

Alongside her birth mother, there were other mother figures that we also explored. Alexia had experienced two foster mothers during her childhood. She had a difficult experience in her first foster placement, perhaps made harder for her with the emergence of Angry Doll. Alexia acknowledged that she was not easy to care for at this time; I heard of a foster experience where her needs were not understood. The move into a long-term foster placement gave Alexia a more positive experience of foster care. Her foster parents were committed to caring for Alexia long-term. This also coincided with the emergence of Golden Doll; Alexia was learning to offer compliance instead of anger, to hide herself away. This did not mean her foster parents worried less about her, but it did make her easier to care for. Alexia became expert at hiding her needs. She was burying her longing as a consequence. She was learning to please, and despite the best of intentions this pleasing was not always challenged.

When we reflected on Alexia's experience of foster care, I experienced some difficulties. Alexia was helping me to view foster care through the eyes of someone who was care experienced and could reflect on this experience. I had had some indirect professional contact with the network surrounding Alexia's foster carers when she was living with them, and this made some of these reflections uncomfortable for me. I was aware this could lead to some defensiveness within me. I needed to stay accepting of Alexia's emotions about this, knowing that we were not focusing on what had or hadn't happened, but on Alexia's experience of it.

I was also confronted with the reality of only seeing what we see when working with clients, and not always knowing the experience of others involved. There was nothing unsafe in the long-term foster care that Alexia experienced. Her foster parents were committed to her and motivated to care well for her. Alexia's experience helped me to understand in a very vivid way what I had known in theory: that foster carers choose this role for a reason, and oftentimes this is wrapped up with their own past experiences. Alexia experienced the foster mother's motivation to foster as conditional. This gave me cause to reflect. As I have developed as a DDP therapist I have understood more the depth of the work we need to do with the parents raising children outside of the birth family about what has brought them to parenting. I needed to think about this between sessions, to understand better the complex feelings that I was experiencing through my work with Alexia. This self-reflection was important so that I could stay present with Alexia during sessions. I could then support her as she reached her own understanding of growing up in foster care. I needed to ensure that this was not contaminated in any way by my own experience or beliefs.

Alongside this revisiting of the past, Alexia was continuing with present relationships, with her siblings, foster parents and her birth father. The therapeutic work was having an impact upon these relationships. Alexia identified how the work was helping her to find herself, but in the process, she feared losing others. Alexia was beginning to recognise the needs she held. She was becoming open to getting these needs met, even when this conflicted with what others needed from her. She agonised over this. She wanted to put her own needs first whilst not wanting to be selfish or manipulative with others. She struggled with what was reasonable and what was unreasonable. Again, she needed to find some balance between these two positions, avoiding the pull back to sacrificing her own needs in order to meet what others wanted from her.

We moved from past to present or present to past within our sessions. I witnessed these developing relationships, handled in an increasingly mature way by Alexia. It took her courage and strength not to be pulled back into old ways of being, allowing healthier relationships to emerge in the process. Alexia worried about losing these relationships. She talked eloquently about the realistic fear that in finding herself she would lose others. She worked hard to be true to herself whilst trying to bring others along with her. I witnessed a young woman who was developing the maturity and confidence to leave behind who she had been and to discover who she was: a maturity and confidence that recognised the impact this was having on people close to her. She had the strength to change these relationships, inviting others to enter a reciprocal relationship with her. Whether they would be able to do this was not in her gift; all she could do was extend the invitation. She remained available and willing to engage with them on reciprocal terms if they chose to accept this invitation. She was aware of the sadness she experienced when they could not. She was prepared to lose relationships in order to be true to herself. She held on to hope that over time the relationships would change rather than be lost.

One of these relationships was with her birth father. Alexia was pleased to be rediscovering a relationship with him. She needed all her new-found flexibility to manage this. She was trying to understand his past behaviour, whilst finding an adult relationship with him. This required her to confront her own idealised image of the good parent. This was a different exploration to that with her birth mother because she was having an ongoing relationship with him in the present, whilst remembering the relationship from the past.

As we had been exploring, Alexia did not experience a parent able to meet all her needs as an infant and small child. She went on to experience the losses of her parents, and later foster carers. By the time she entered long-term foster care Alexia did not know what a parent should or could be. She grieved the lack of an unconditional parent in her life. As part of this grieving process Alexia was also confronting what she wanted and expected from parents. We discovered that, for her, this meant a parent who was perfect, loving unconditionally, without rupture. Alexia was grieving the loss of an idealised image of a parent alongside the real losses she had experienced.

Together we explored the fallibility in all of us. We reflected on the ruptures in our relationship that had occurred within sessions and which I had taken responsibility to repair. She experienced relationship ruptures with Andrew and his family, and how willing they were to repair these. Less black and white now, Alexia was able to notice the difference between what she had believed and what she was discovering; the complex mixture of fallible and infallible that makes us all human. Alexia's idea of a good parent was changing. It was not about perfection. She was understanding the importance of a parent being willing to privilege the relationship, repairing ruptures as they arise. Alexia's birth father was able to do this, and together, Alexia and I were able to appreciate this.

During this whole phase of therapy Alexia's grieving was intense. I witnessed the healing power of this grieving. Uncomfortable as it was to experience, without this she could not come to terms with the losses and the longings in her life. She could not find peace. I could see signs of developing health. Alexia was physically feeling better, eating well and maintaining good self-care. We also noticed her migraines reducing as she was holding on to less repressed emotion. Alexia was growing in resilience.

Alexia would need as much resilience as she could find as we moved into the most difficult phase of the therapy. We had avoided this so far. I have wondered whether this was because of avoidance on both our parts, or was in recognition of the resilience that she needed to build first. Perhaps it was a bit of both, but

I can't claim that the progression of therapy was foreseen, thought out or planned by me. Unconscious forces guided us both, and human fallibility held us back at times. When I look back on the course of the therapy it unfolded in a logical way, from easier to more difficult; from lighter to deeper; from outside to inside; and yes, inevitably to the hardest experience of all.

Armoured by Loss: The Princess' Tale

Why do we so often run from grief as if it is a harsh companion that we will not tolerate? We do anything to escape from it even though we can lose ourselves in the process. Why is it so hard to believe that there is comfort in acceptance? A comfort that is found in learning to live with grief. This is the story of Princess Alexandra and her struggle to find a way to live with the grief of a loss that was there even at her beginning.

Queen Beatrice was born into wealth and luxury but without love. Her parents ruled their land harshly and brought Beatrice up in the same way. When she ascended to the throne, she was determined to be different. She sought the love of her people and indeed they looked up to her as a kind, generous and beneficent ruler; a contrast to the years of tyranny they had endured. When she had a child, she had another opportunity. She could show her people what a kind and caring mother she was. And indeed, that is what they saw. Queen Beatrice knew how to put on a show. She did love her little girl, as far as she was able, but this was a love of conditions. As long as Alexandra fulfilled her role in portraying a loved and cherished child all was well, but if Alexandra made her own needs felt everything changed. Queen Beatrice needed her but had little to give in return.

In the beginning Alexandra protested. An infant has few ways to signal her needs, and when these wear her parent out what else can she do? Alexandra cried and her mother despaired. She resented these demands, which left her feeling useless and unappreciated. She needed her child to be quiet and calm. She needed to show her to the people so that they would love her as the good mother she would like to be.

Alexandra learned not to cry, and an uneasy peace descended upon them. She sought ways to gain the love of her mother. She learned to be what her mother needed her to be. Alexandra had put on the first layer of armour and a little bit of her was lost in the process.

Alexandra grew into a bonny child. The people fussed over her whilst her mother looked away. Alexandra followed her mother, anxious to gain her approval, desperate to feel the love and pride of a mother for her daughter. This rarely happened. When she fell, she was chastised as clumsy. When she strayed, she was punished as naughty. When she tore her clothes, she was berated as careless.

Alexandra learned not to fall, not to stray, and not to tear her clothes. She learned to care for her mother, always attentive to what she needed, always anxious not to displease. But she was only a child; her care could not be good enough, and displeasure would happen despite her best efforts. She spent many hours locked in her room when she failed again to be what her mother needed. Then her mother would return with pretty clothes and toys. She fussed over her daughter, dressing her and brushing her hair. Alexandra was confused as they went out together. Gone was the angry, demanding mother. In its place was a mother who could not do enough for her - as long as the people watched. By evening Alexandra would be alone again. Alexandra learned not to take pleasure in her mother's attention. She learned not to be disappointed in her mother's absence, forming a second layer of armour as another part of herself was lost.

A tutor was employed to educate the growing Alexandra. He instructed her in her lessons and taught her the royal arts. She learned how to entertain and to parley. She learned how to ride, hunt and use a sword. Alexandra enjoyed these lessons. She liked to make her tutor proud. Her mother watched her daughter grow close to the tutor. The next day he was gone, and another took his place. Alexandra learned her lessons. Alexandra learned not to grow close to her tutors. Another layer of armour fell into place.

The adolescent Alexandra was both beautiful and accomplished. She was also empty inside. She remained attentive to her mother's demands, tuned in to her needs and careful not to betray any needs of her own. This was not enough; her mother would take to her chambers, sometimes for weeks at a time. Alexandra learned to run the household. She learned to go out into the lands to hear the wishes of the people. She was loved by all but cherished by none. Alexandra appeared beautiful, kind and helpful. Alexandra was hidden. Everyone saw in her what they wanted to see. Her armour reflected their need of her. And still her mother was not satisfied. She resented Alexandra for all that she did. She feared that Alexandra would surpass her. Queen Beatrice needed the people to love her, not Alexandra.

A new child was born. This child would be what her mother needed. Queen Beatrice could again show her people what a kind and loving mother she was. They would not look for Alexandra when they saw this new child growing in her care.

Alexandra tried to please her mother. Alexandra tried to protect her brother. Queen Beatrice was not satisfied. Alexandra was sent away to defend their land from a neighbouring kingdom. Her armour complete and mounted on a horse as sad as she was, she rode away with her soldiers to try to meet this new demand of her mother.

'Do not return until you have driven them back from our borders,' she was told.

Alexandra despaired. They were outnumbered and outskilled. Her soldiers looked to her for guidance, but she was young, not battle hardened. Although she fought bravely, she made mistakes and defeat came closer. She rode ahead, desperate to meet this challenge, desperate to please her mother. As a stray arrow pierced her armour, she knew she had failed. She lay on the ground, her faithful horse protecting her.

She was found many hours later. A parley had been held; a peace restored. The prince returning to his kingdom noticed her horse and rode up to investigate. Dismounting, he knelt next to her, relieved to see that she was still breathing. He marvelled at her courage, her bravery, her beauty. Gently he put her on her horse and brought her back to the palace. He was determined to restore her to health.

Alexandra's wounds healed, and her strength returned. The

prince was attentive. He ensured that she had all that she needed. There was one thing that he could not give her, however. Alexandra had failed and her heart was breaking. She couldn't please her mother and win the love she longed for.

Alexandra did the only thing she knew: she buried her despair, her grief. She turned to the prince and thanked him for all he had done. She offered her loyalty in turn. Fearing to go home, she lingered at his palace. They took to walking the grounds together. They talked of much and little. They discovered companionship even whilst Alexandra protected the hidden parts of herself.

This was a time of both peace and uncertainty for Alexandra. She enjoyed this newly found friendship but feared the loss of it. She sought to please the prince, searching for what he needed whilst hiding her own need away.

The prince in turn had his own uncertainties. He wanted to rescue Alexandra and give her what she longed for. He searched for what was hidden despite her protests. Even whilst their friendship deepened, these differing needs lay between them. The prince did not want to be pleased; he wanted to be loved. Alexandra did not want to be found; she sought to stay hidden. They talked of a life together, but Alexandra was not yet ready to give up on her mother's love. She still yearned to find a way back to her.

Their daily walks grew longer as they both found comfort in the forest around the castle. They loved seeing the forest in different weathers. They loved glimpses of the creatures they found there. There was a freedom here that they could not find elsewhere. As they moved more deeply in, they entered areas the prince had never explored. He did not know it, but they were being drawn into an enchanted part of the forest. This enchantment gave wisdom to all those who passed through. They lingered here for the longest time, intuitively knowing that this is where they needed to be. They talked of a future that they both wanted, and of the fears that threatened to get in the way. They both knew that they would have to give up something first.

The prince needed to learn both to care and to be cared for. Only then would there be balance in their relationship. He told her he would do this willingly. As long as she was patient with him, he would find a way. Alexandra knew patience would be no problem but still she held back.

'I think I want this, but I am so afraid,' she told him. 'I have spent so many years pleasing others I am no longer sure who I am or what I want. My armour has protected me, but I lost myself behind it. I no longer know what it is shielding, but I fear to give it up.'

'Then we will look together,' he said. 'Trust me and I will help you remove the armour and be free at last.'

'It might make me free, but I fear what I might lose,' she protested. 'What if you see me and it is not enough? What if you don't like the Me we find? After all, my mother was never satisfied. There must be something wrong with me. You look at me and see only the armour. It reflects back what you want to see. I am scared to find out who I really am.'

The prince wanted to say that this could not be. He wanted to reassure Alexandra that he would always love her whatever was revealed. Wisdom held him back. Wisdom told him to go slowly, to truly understand and accept Alexandra's fears. Stay with her and help her to face these fears. Help her to find herself.

And so, the prince asked Alexandra to tell him of her life, her experiences, her triumphs and her failures. They sat under a tree as the sun grew lower and the moon began to rise. Alexandra told of a baby who cried but who was not answered, a toddler who tried but got so much wrong, a child who learned to hide her own needs and take care of others and an adolescent who despite all her efforts had lost what she had always been seeking. She had never been good enough, try as hard as she could. She believed that there was some part of her that was so bad it denied her a mother's love.

The prince listened with much empathy and no judgement. Gently he removed the armour to find the true self within.

Alexandra felt exposed by his acceptance. She felt undone by his empathy. She looked away for fear of what she would see revealed in his eyes. She felt certain only disgust would be there. She longed to run; to leave behind his eyes that seemed in that moment to look just like her mother's.

'You cannot love me,' she cried. 'I am not good enough for you.'

She could hear her mother's voice, berating her. She was lazy, no good; she would not amount to anything. And then confusion, her mother was holding her, whispering kind words to her, telling the people of her clever, beautiful daughter.

'I am trying, Mother,' she cried. 'I am trying to be clever and beautiful for you. I am trying to look after you, defend you, be with you as you need me to be.'

The prince held her. 'Look at me,' he said. 'It is me, not your mother. I am here. I see you and I love you for who you are. You feel bad, but I see a crying baby, a hurt toddler, a hidden child and an adolescent trying to find out who she is. Let me find out with you.'

She saw him then and knew he spoke the truth.

'I am scared,' she said. 'I can't be myself and also what she wants me to be. If I find myself then I fear I will lose her. I thought if I could be perfect, she would come to me. Now I see that all I did was hide myself. I showed her what she wanted and still it wasn't enough. Can I let her go? Can I be me?'

'I don't know,' the prince said. 'But we can find out together.'

The following weeks were some of the hardest of Alexandra's life. She had a well of grief inside her that she feared would consume her. She rode out alone within the enchanted forest, her faithful horse her only companion. She cried a stream of tears so deep she thought she would drown. She knew she could not have what she had always wanted. She also understood that it wasn't her fault. In giving up this deception she also gave up a dream. Her mother could not give her what she needed, no matter what she did. She emerged sadder but stronger and more real than she had ever been. At last, she went to the prince and he smiled.

'I see you,' he said, as they walked arm in arm, their future ahead of them.

Grief remained a companion to Alexandra, but it was a grief she could bear. She would always remember what she didn't have, and in accepting this she found wisdom and comfort. Loss was at her beginning and it accompanied her always. In accepting her loss she gained more than she ever imagined, and finally this was enough.

Chapter 8

MENDING THE KINTSUGI POT

FINDING ME

I think it is done. I am ready to move forward in my life. I look towards an ending. And then suddenly it is there. The hardest thing of all. We have more to do. I am devastated.

It starts with humiliation and leads us to abuse. I am powerless. I am a victim. He stands over me. I feel intruded upon in every way. I am contaminated. My childhood was contaminated. I am damaged goods. I don't tell. I cannot break my aunt's heart. That is how he controls me.

Mother could not give me what I needed. I had Dad and Auntie. That made it easier.

With him it is different. Not entirely my fault, but I am to blame. Or so I believe. I am a cracked pot and cannot be put back together again. I was so little when it started. I was frozen. Am I to blame?

I dream of rejection from all who love me. I am damaged. I cannot let others see this. I make myself attractive to hide.

I make myself strong to protect myself. I cannot just be. This impacts on my relationship with my husband. I want normal.

I need to remember. I need to tell my story. There is a black hole within me. I don't know what I don't remember. I forgot for so long. The memories came back all at once. But do I have them all?

I loved my aunt. She didn't know. I tried to tell her, but he used words that made it sound innocent. I was so little. I didn't know what to tell. It felt so dangerous. I tried to be good. I didn't say no. I felt he would kill me. Does this make it my fault? I didn't fight. I didn't run. Did this save my life? I remember what he did. The games. The secrecy. I took these games to my playmates, my sister, my dolls. I did not understand. I was little. I could not make sense of it.

I remember but I don't feel. I am numb. I feel sick. I feel tight in my chest. I remember the tiger. It is not only my mother. It is also him! It is dangerous. I have to placate it. I feel fire in my legs. I want to run. It is dangerous to run.

I dream about the tiger. I am bigger and stronger. I can protect myself now. I lock the door. He can no longer reach me.

I am angry. I imagine telling him of my anger, my contempt. I feel like screaming, but it is so hard to let this out. I imagine standing in a field and screaming all that I feel at the top of my voice.

I do not feel ashamed any more. I was little. It was wrong. It was not my fault. I am proud of the cracks; they have made me who I am. Not a broken pot but beautiful and whole. We discover Kintsugi. This is me. From Russian Doll to Kintsugi pot, made whole.

Reflections from Alexia

It is hard to reflect on this part of the therapy. As then, I feel it needs to be done but I don't want to do it. It is hard to remember. I was emotional, but I was also frozen and stuck. I could talk about the abuse, keep it in my head; we had done this earlier. Feeling it was something else. How to reflect on the emotional work we did, when so much was feeling without thought. Realising that I needed to do this work felt catastrophic, and as I reflect on this now, I feel there is still more to do.

I had convinced myself that if we did the attachment work, making sense of why adults couldn't keep me safe, I wouldn't need to face the abuse. My hope was that in finding safety in attachment relationships I would gain enough resilience to go forward without the need to look back at this part of my life. I was trying to protect myself from having to expose my most shameful parts to Kim. I was back to the feeling that all would be lost if I showed these parts of myself. I was convinced that this time Kim would not be able to handle it. She would find me disgusting and she would send me away. In my head there was no other option – this was very certain to me.

However, I was drowning. On the surface all seemed fine, but underneath the waters of my shame and disgust were threatening to engulf me. On top of this, my relationship with Andrew was at stake. The impact of the abuse was getting in the way. Somewhere within me I knew this. I needed to find a way to swim, not drown. Some part of me must have recognised this even whilst I was trying to deny it. An unconscious part of me needed to let Kim know.

Just like at the beginning of therapy I began by discussing a work context. I had no awareness of the deeper significance of this. I was simply relating a troubling experience at work when I had felt humiliated by colleagues. I knew this felt big, but I had no idea what it meant. This in itself was unusual as I am a reflective person. The fact I couldn't make sense of what I had experienced was a red flag. I needed help to sort this out.

It was like a dot-to-dot picture, only I couldn't see the dots, never mind the picture. If the dots weren't available to me, how could I figure out the meaning? Without realising it I took the dots to Kim and she joined them up for me.

When Kim said that this was about needing to work on the sexual abuse, it felt catastrophic. It also felt obvious. Of course, this made absolute sense. It was time to face something that had haunted me all my life. In confronting this I felt I was risking losing everything and everybody, but there was no other option. If I didn't do this, I might lose myself. I had to take the risk.

This was hard. I felt like I wouldn't survive the telling but also that survival depended on me doing this. I felt I was about to expose my cracks and I would shatter into a million pieces. I would disintegrate, become dust, utterly annihilated. I was trapped, feeling like I couldn't tell but also like I couldn't not tell. It felt impossible, there seemed to be no way out and I felt beaten. I left this session feeling that I didn't care if I lived or died. This was the only time I felt like this. I remember driving home fast, recklessly. It just didn't matter; everything was going to be lost anyway. When I got home, I slept and slept. Until the next session I was just existing. I was floating, numb, no feelings, just existence.

I had no hesitation about coming back for the next session. I knew that Kim would take care of me, and I needed this. Notice, reader, how confusing this is. I was certain that she would reject me. I was also certain that she would take care of me. This was disorganising. I was in chaos. I brought this paradox to Kim. I was holding two contradictory beliefs. They could not exist together. When Kim showed compassion for what I believed were the most disgusting parts of myself, the paradox was resolved. I could no longer hold on to both beliefs, and the fear that I was so disgusting she would abandon me began to disappear. Over the next few sessions I was able to tell the story of what had happened to me and to share the most shameful parts of this. In the telling the shame went. I no longer blamed myself. I was now ready to work with my anger towards the abuser.

I felt a burning rage towards him. How dare he have hurt me? I was a child and I deserved better. Kim helped me to tell him this using the empty chair. I felt powerful, I was choosing to take control. I wasn't going to let him hurt me any more. I was no longer a victim to the experience or to the memories that I had lived with every day. This was pivotal. I finally accepted myself as a survivor.

Of all the stories that Kim wrote for me, my favourite is 'The Kintsugi Pot'. This felt even more me. It was the first time that sexual abuse was acknowledged. It was accepted as being a part of my experience and it was not shameful. I loved the idea of the Kintsugi pot. It was so beautiful. Not only could a pot be fixed, but fixed in a way that made the cracks beautiful; it was fixed with gold. This sums up all the work we did over the three years; healing without the need for perfection. I could really identify with being Pot. I don't know why, but it felt right. The story was really helpful, and it was really painful. I remember being frightened to read this story. It felt like a risk. Would I be judged? Would Kim have written something shameful about me? I couldn't imagine this story being told without it being shameful. When I read the story, there was no shame; the cracks weren't bad. I had believed the abuse was all my fault; the story helped me to see that it wasn't. This had happened, and others were responsible.

Reflections from Kim

Alexia was increasingly having nightmares with themes of being in danger. Amongst these nightmares an image of a tiger kept appearing. Earlier, Alexia had identified the image of a tiger with her mother. We now had to revisit this image, finding another very different connection.

It was whilst we were catching up that we were confronted with the next phase of our work. Alexia told me of some experiences she had been having at work and elsewhere that she was finding concerning. She was puzzled about why she was reacting so strongly to situations with colleagues. She described these situations and how they left her feeling humiliated. This feeling was so strong and unpleasant that she needed to leave the room at times. She wanted to understand why these relatively benign situations were having such a strong impact upon her. I wondered about the word 'humiliation' that she had used. What did this word mean to her? What was being humiliated like for Alexia? As she talked about her work experience, she described humiliation as feeling victimised, powerless and a sense of someone having control over her. She associated this especially with men or boys. As I explored this further with her, she described an image of someone bigger standing over her. She noticed how intrusive this felt.

I had a strong feeling as I listened to her. The meaning was obvious to me, although not yet to Alexia. She was feeling relaxed and confident. Confident that the hard work was behind her. Comfortable in her newfound sense of who she was and where she was going. I was about to turn this newly discovered world upside down. We had more work to do.

Inevitably we arrived where we needed to be. There was a further piece of the puzzle that was Alexia. I needed to help her to work through the trauma of sexual abuse. This was something that I should have been ready for, but I think its arrival on this day took us both by surprise. We had explored this earlier in the work, and I think a naïve part of myself had hoped that this was sufficient. As we explored her experience of feeling humiliated, I realised that there was a deeper meaning to this experience, one associated with the trauma of the sexual abuse she remembered experiencing. As the realisation hit me that Alexia was ready to work with this trauma, I rather sprung this upon her. This was distressing for Alexia. She thought we were done with the hard things. She now realised that even harder work was ahead of her. I watched Alexia crumple in front of me, as she cried and protested a world that just kept getting harder. To say she was devastated is probably an understatement. She didn't want any more pain. She wanted it to be over. She wanted to move forward with her life, the therapy behind her. She knew that therapy was about to get a whole lot harder.

I sat with her, my presence steadying her, as it had done many times before. I agreed that this was unfair. She had worked so hard. She deserved a rest. Together we would get through this as we had worked through so much before. Alexia, small again and frightened, looked at me. 'Was this it?' her eyes told me. Was this the thing that would lead to her being found out? Was I about to find out the bad at the core of her, the contamination that would make me abandon her at last? All I could do was let her know that I understood. Her fears made sense to me. We would explore these together as we had explored so many fears before. She told me that she was a cracked pot and could not be mended. I empathised with how scary this thought was. What a hard belief to have lived with all these years. No wonder she often felt she was close to losing everything.

My whole focus was on Alexia; on holding her safe. I needed her to feel my presence, and to know I was not going to run away from her. Inside I was needing to put aside my own reaction to this: my strong impulse was to run away; not from Alexia and not with disgust. This was an uncomfortable area for me to work with. For now, I needed to hold my story in the background whilst I attended to what Alexia needed. Later, sexual abuse would enter my dreams. I would need to explore this and my own discomfort with sexual abuse during supervision. I needed to be held so that I could continue to offer to Alexia what she needed at this time.

I felt huge compassion for Alexia and wanted to offer her some hope which would help her to confront this with her usual courage and resilience. This was not to dismiss her experience but would help us to sit with it with the confidence that we would find a way through. Alexia had described herself as a cracked pot, and this brought to my mind the Japanese art of Kintsugi. This was to become our hopeful symbol to carry her through this part of the work. I bought her a Christmas present, a small piece of Kintsugi jewellery to help her to hold onto this symbol.

The giving of gifts is something that is not always considered acceptable in some therapy models. Within DDP there is a recognition that the relationship is at the heart of the work, and carefully considered gifts are seen as appropriate gestures. With Alexia I used gifts as a way of demonstrating connection during breaks in therapy, and, as in this case, as symbols of our work together.

And so, we embarked on the final piece of Alexia's story: the heart of the trauma she had experienced. We started with the telling of the story, going slowly to give sufficient time and space for processing and integration. Supervision held me steady so that Alexia and I could move level by level through the story, starting with the easier elements and progressing to the more difficult, more shameful parts.

Even with strong acceptance from me, Alexia experienced a high level of shame whilst telling this story. At times she could barely look at me. She feared what my look would communicate: that I too believed she was contaminated, with no way back. At my instruction she would look briefly at me, long enough to see that I held no blame or judgement towards her. She needed a lot of co-regulation as we moved towards the hardest parts of her story. She needed to feel my full acceptance if she was ever going to find her own. Alexia persevered in the telling. She knew she needed to do this, even whilst she was dreading the consequences. Over a few sessions she told her story, including what were to her the most shameful elements. Only when it was told could she relax. The worst was done; what would be, would be.

One of the earliest things Alexia said to me during this telling was that she was not entirely to blame for what had happened. That word – 'entirely' – told its own story. Alexia could recognise that abuse was not the victim's fault. She could not relate this to herself. She was to blame for it happening; she was to blame for not saying no; she was to blame for freezing instead of fighting or running; she was to blame for placating. This was particularly hard to hear, given how young she was when the abuse began. I was reminded of her strong feelings towards Baby Doll, and the blame this most vulnerable part of her had held for so long.

Alexia told me that this period of the work invaded her life. She felt like she was having a breakdown. Alongside this she was having dreams of rejection from a range of people, familiar and not. Her fear that in this story was the heart of her contamination, the core of her badness, was palpable.

There were times when Alexia felt like retreating behind her mask again, to return to the defensive strategies that she had moved away from. My continuing acceptance made this hard for her to do. She told me that my acceptance was the Achilles heel of the mask. I marvelled at how clearly she could articulate her experience, in just a few words. She recognised that she could not maintain the mask without rejecting me and what I was offering to her.

I listened and did not judge and gradually the telling changed. Alexia began to see herself as victim. She moved from blame and condemnation to understanding that she was blameless. We realised, at last, that the tiger that haunted her dreams was also the abuser. It was time to metaphorically confront the abuser. It was time for Alexia to stand up for herself.

We returned to the empty chair for the final part of this piece of the work. This time the chair represented the abuser. Initially I talked for her, helping her to find the courage to talk to him. She then found her own words to tell of all that she felt about him and what he had done to her. Her chest tightened and her breathing shallowed as she took control back. Her resilience was there as she talked confidently and with authority to the chair/abuser. No diffidence now. No questioning whether this was okay. She knew without doubt that what he had done was wrong and she wanted him to know it too. I didn't need to talk for her any more. She had found her own voice.

I could see that a lot was going on physically for Alexia whilst she was working with this experientially. I asked her to tell me what she felt. She noticed that her legs were becoming hot, feeling an urge to run. Elsewhere, she noticed feeling numb. We thought about the small child who felt like running but who could not move. I invited her to run in the garden, but she felt too self-conscious. I wished we had a bigger space to help her do some of the body work that she needed to do.

Alexia also felt a strong desire to shout her anger. I suggested she go ahead, but this was too hard. A part of her feared angering him still. When she was little, she had felt her life threatened by him. Vestiges of this fear remained within her, inhibiting her. She was cross with herself that she could not find the voice to do this. We used visualisation to help her with this. I don't think that this felt entirely satisfactory. Later she would dream of taking control. She dreamt she was strong enough to lock the tiger out of the room she was in, her dreams allowing her to finish the work we started in these sessions.

Alongside this work I also thought with Alexia about the impact of this abuse on her relationship with Andrew. We identified the importance of couples work to help them both. We also agreed that I would not be the right person to do this work. My role was therapist to Alexia, and as a symbolic mother figure we both agreed that this would not be comfortable. I was also feeling unskilled for this work as it is not an area of expertise for me. We agreed that I would help her to find someone else who they could go to and that she and Andrew would decide when the time felt right.

The Kintsugi Pot

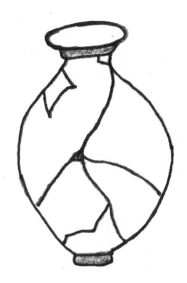

*Kintsugi represents the Japanese art of repairing broken
pottery. Kintsugi (金継ぎ) means 'golden joinery'. It is also
known as Kintsukuroi (金繕い): 'golden repair'. The broken
parts of the pot are repaired with a lacquer dusted or mixed
with powdered gold, silver or platinum. This art honours
the pot; the breakage and subsequent repair are viewed as
part of its history rather than something to disguise.*

Pot thinks that there was some tenderness at her creation, although it is hard for her to imagine this. She was carefully crafted by the couple who fashioned her with a design that was unique and beautiful. She also remembers being handled carefully, put out on the table when visitors came; but she did not have a purpose – she was on display but not useful. Pot wanted to be useful, she wanted to please, to be a good pot. When the visitors went, she found herself back on the shelf, abandoned and neglected. It was hard for her to feel loved and wanted. Over time two other pots were made and joined her on the shelf. Pot liked having the company, but she was also jealous. What if one of them was taken down and not her? What if one of them was useful?

As time went by, Pot became more anxious. She feared she would never be loved and cherished as a pot needed to be. Sometimes she would feel angry. She would shout at the other pots. Most of all she just wanted to please. With all these mixed-up feelings, small cracks appeared on her surface. Pot despaired. How would anyone love her now? Anyone looking at her could see she was no good. Pot moved further back on the shelf, hiding away as best she could.

One day Pot heard people in the house. A good-looking couple. Pot could see them. There was a motherly looking woman who spoke quietly and kindly. Pot wished this lady might notice her. She inched forward so that she could get a better look. The man was different. He had a gruff voice, and he frightened Pot. She didn't know why, but she didn't like him. She was just retreating to the back of the shelf when she was noticed. The man reached up and pulled her out.

'Here,' the man said. 'This one will do.'

He handed her to the lady, who he called Auntie. She cradled the pot to her.

'Yes,' she said. 'This is perfect. May I borrow her? I promise I will take good care of her.'

And so, it was decided. Pot went home with Auntie and the

man. This was a time of much conflict for Pot. She loved being with Auntie. She felt truly cared for, and indeed useful as Auntie let her hold all sorts of wonderful things. She was admired by anyone visiting the house, but not discarded when they left. Auntie liked to keep her close and Pot enjoyed these times. Sometimes, however, the man took hold of her. This was scary. He was rougher than Auntie, although he spoke to her kindly. Pot did not know what to make of him, but she wanted to stay with Auntie. She decided that the safest thing was to make herself as useful as she could. If she pleased them both, maybe everything would be okay.

Pot tried her best, and indeed she seemed to be appreciated. The man called her special and admired her beauty. He would sit with Pot on his lap and would fill her up. But this was not the same as Auntie. Pot found she didn't like this attention. He hurt her, and it felt all wrong. Pot did not think he was kind, and worried that he might even break her. Indeed, some of his rough handling was forming deeper cracks in her pottery. Pot did not know what to do. She didn't dare to be angry with him, for fear he would hurt her even more. She tried to please him, but this just led to even more horrid attention from him. The only relief she got was when she was back with Auntie again. She could relax with her, enjoy the comfort that she brought. Pot wished that Auntie would keep her to herself; protect her from the man. Why didn't Auntie notice what was happening?

This continued for many years. Pot moved home several times, but always she would be lent to Auntie and the man. Pot did the best she could. She tried to behave as a good pot. She tried to be useful and to please. Only with Auntie, though, did she ever feel truly appreciated and cared for. Only with the man did she ever feel really frightened. This was all too hard. Inside Pot shut down. She did not know what to do, and so she did the only thing that she could. She stopped feeling what was happening. The cracks got deeper but Pot could not feel them any more.

Pot did not realise, but as time went by she was growing

stronger. Little by little she was learning to take control of her life. She still wanted to please and to be useful, but a part of her was also learning to rebel. At first, she would assert herself in little ways. She would not show her best side. She would not allow herself to hold pleasant treats or useful tools. She was careful about this. On the outside she still appeared to be a good and useful pot, but inside she was learning to be someone quite different. She learnt to manage without being cared for. Finally, she even learned to manage without Auntie. She would not go and see Auntie and the man any more. She did have a little hope that maybe Auntie would find her and keep her safe, but this didn't happen, and Pot found that it did not matter. She could manage on her own. She learnt to bury the longing to be cared for. She was an independent pot.

Pot was successful. She forgot all about the man. She learnt not to miss Auntie. She grew clever. She even made friends. Pot discovered that she could still be admired. This puzzled Pot. How could this be with all the cracks she now had? Surely others would notice what a broken pot she was?

There was one special friend whom she spent a lot of time with. Pot found herself trusting him. She told him about being cracked and her fears that no-one would like her. She even remembered about the man and told him about her fear of him. Pot thought that her friend would not want to be with her when he knew all this. He would see her for what she was: a pot who was bad and had lots of cracks. A contaminated pot. She was surprised when he did not seem to mind. He told her she would always be a beautiful pot to him. He wanted her to see herself as he saw her. Pot did not believe that this was possible. She would always know what she was.

This friend knew a person who made beautiful pots. He suggested they go to see her and get her advice. Pot was scared. This lady might say she was too ugly. She might not want to help her. Pot was also brave. She decided to go and see her despite her fears. The lady was kind and caring. She gently took Pot and examined her all over, inside and out. She learnt about her story and looked at all the cracks and marks that were left on her.

Pot asked, 'Can you make the cracks go away?'

The lady smiled. 'Why would I want to do that? Those cracks make you the strong, brave pot that you have become. They are part of you. They make you unique. I will take care of the cracks, but I won't make them go away. You will see – you will be more beautiful than ever once I have taken care of them.'

The lady collected together her tools and some liquid gold. She gently broke the pot into pieces, guided by the cracks, and then carefully and tenderly glued them back together using lacquered resin made from the gold. She worked carefully, ensuring that all the cracks and scratches were attended to. She worked through many days. She did not rush. When Pot needed a break they both rested. Pot was still worried about the cracks and how everyone would see them. She found it so hard to believe that others could love her with these cracks.

As time went on she began to feel stronger; more whole. She didn't need to hide any more. She didn't need to shut down and not feel anything. She could be herself and show herself to others. By the time the lady had finished she could almost believe she was beautiful. She would always worry about the cracks, but she was proud of herself all the same.

Pot imagined there had been tenderness at her creation; she experienced it at her renewal. Through this process she learnt to accept all the difficult times in her life and to discover the strength and courage it had given her. She was a beautiful, unique and amazing pot who loved and was loved in turn.

Chapter 9

BRINGING ANDREW
INTO THE WORK

FINDING ME

He has been a part of me for so long. I need him as I need no other; he is my partner, friend and support. He rescued me. And yet, even as I recognise this need, I reject it. He cannot help me. I control this too. I do not let him in when I need him the most. I cannot allow him to find my truth: that I am wrong. He is with me and it is the loneliest I have been. I fear staying the same. I fear losing him. Can we both change? Is he part of this process? The thought is terrifying.

Something in me is changing. I am losing the control I have held onto for so long. I need him more than I have needed anyone. I show him this. It feels a risk, but I cannot help it. Am I going to wear him out? I pull him in; find me, notice me, accept me. I push him away; go, don't stay. Will you stay? Don't let me burn you out. He comes to therapy. It is torture. I cannot look at him. See me. Don't see me. This is who I am. Will you leave me now? He stays.

We find each other. It is hard. It is scary. It is real. Our relationship changes as we discover we need each other. We search for balance. We search for joy. We learn to talk when these are missing. We discover our stories together and this makes us stronger.

Reflections from Andrew

Prior to Alexia's therapy with Kim, she made it obvious to me that her intention was to receive help with finding herself and working on her acceptance. I was a huge supporter of this, always having known and witnessed her struggle to be her true self, mostly with others, as I at the time felt I had her true self. Which I still believe I did, just parts of it, not all of it.

Going into therapy sessions I had very few expectations and no idea what to anticipate; coming from a past where I was in the habit of putting up and shutting up, it made me nervous. Nervous, but not threatened, as I knew this was firstly for Alexia and I wanted to help her and this journey. I remember Kim asking me, one to one, what my attachment history was like and I had no idea what to say; I felt surprised that Kim was asking about me, as I thought this was meant to be for Alexia. At this time I believed my childhood had no challenges. As time went on, I learnt that I lacked intent to explore both mine and Alexia's true thoughts and emotions of any given moment, both in therapy or in the past, and even found it uncomfortable. Recognising this helped me understand I had room to grow also.

Kim's guidance in the sessions, particularly early on, was vital for me. When given the opportunity to speak to Alexia for the first time during our first session together, I vividly remember going for the default silver lining, completely missing the point of understanding how to be a part of Alexia's feelings and be empathetic towards them. Not that I wasn't, I just didn't have the conscious ability to go there straight away. With some help from Kim about what sort of questions and responses should follow these really tough conversations they were going through together, I started to understand that I could, and should, experience the hardship, sadness and loss both for myself and for my wife.

When I was first introduced to the room, Alexia struggled to have the conversations she had been having; it was obviously threatening and more painful for her than I had ever seen. All I wanted to do was grab her in my arms and silver line things. But to sit and witness, and to let her know I was there with her, became the most powerful thing I could do.

Over this period of time, Alexia started to recognise, outside of sessions, that she could be her true self. Not yet entirely all at once; it was as if month by month she would test certain parts of herself with me and those around us. Sometimes she would let me and others know she was angry; other months it would be sadness, courage and occasionally a lack of empathy towards others, as her recognition of her own needs and past suffering became more obvious.

Now, she has all of those things and, it would seem, all when appropriately needed. Alexia feels the most rounded and genuine she has ever felt. Still the Alexia I met and fell in love with, only now complete. Our relationship is now one of mutual give and take, the effort has stopped, we continue helping each other explore ourselves together successfully now that we have the tools to do so.

Reflections from Alexia

Even before Andrew came into the sessions, he was part of the work. It was essential to me that Kim so readily accepted Andrew as part of my life. Other significant people in my life had ridiculed and minimised my relationship with him. It felt as if they were rejecting him, and threatening to reject me if I remained with him. I think they experienced him as a threat. It felt as if they wanted me for themselves. I could not have both; I was put in the position of having to choose between them or him.

With Kim it felt as if there was space for more than one relationship. It felt as if Kim was valuing Andrew's importance in my life. This made me feel able to bring everything to Kim, not just the good stuff. I could talk about the beauty and the difficulties in our relationship. These were accepted equally. This gave me an experience of being able to have more than one significant relationship at once. It did not need to be a conflict. It also challenged my idea that relationships had to be all good or all bad. There was more balance.

When Kim suggested bringing Andrew into some of the sessions, I was terrified. At first, I avoided this at all costs. Initially I didn't even tell him that Kim had suggested this. Then I conveniently forgot to give him the dates! I agreed that in theory this was a good idea, but in reality I feared the consequences.

When I met Andrew he quickly became the most important person in my life. He came with the offer of something different. He was a real person who really cared for me. Meeting Andrew was a life-changing event. In hindsight, I asked too much of him: to be partner, friend, parent figure, supporter, defender, rescuer. I therefore had so much to lose if this relationship went wrong. This is why bringing him into sessions felt so threatening. At the same time, a part of me knew that this wasn't sustainable; our relationship had to change and grow alongside my personal growth. Threatening or not, Andrew needed to be part of my therapy journey.

My initial motivation in bringing Andrew along to my sessions was so that he would get the support he needed. I was so afraid that he would burn out and he wouldn't be able to stick with me. Who better to offer this support than Kim? This finally overcame my fear and I brought him along. As ever, the reality was different to what I was anticipating.

This was so much harder than I expected. I couldn't even look at him for fear that he would see me for who I believed I was: bad, not good enough, unlovable. I was so worried that he would no longer want me; that he would leave me. Therapy is full of paradoxes and here was another one. I both wanted parts of me to stay hidden, not known by Andrew, but also wanted him to see the real me. I wanted him to see and accept me. I feared he would see and reject me. Kim knew that I needed to discover that the authentic me was acceptable to him. She helped me to reveal vulnerable parts of me that Andrew had never seen, and this was excruciating. It was therefore surprising to me how close we were after these sessions. I felt connected to him in the most real way we had ever felt. This gave me a glimmer of hope that we could survive whatever was revealed.

It was so hard for me to access my feelings with Andrew there. And yet, Andrew's presence allowed me to get in touch with my most vulnerable feelings in a more real way than when he wasn't there. The additional security that Andrew's presence brought, alongside Kim, meant that Kim could help me experience my deepest worries and fears more intensely than ever before and to experience these being acceptable to them. Spot the paradox again: the increased safety they both provided also came with a double risk. How could it be that both these important people accepted me and didn't throw me away? I sought safety from both of them whilst being scared to death that this safety was imaginary, and I would lose everything.

This was not just about having Andrew in sessions with me. Andrew was a constant in my life, supporting me before, sometimes during, and after sessions. As I was changing through the process of therapy it was inevitable that our relationship had to change as well. We needed to learn how to be a healthier couple. Finding an attachment figure in Kim meant that Andrew was freed from having to be responsible for meeting all my needs. Our relationship became one of reciprocity. Both of us became aware that we needed others in our life, not just each other. This freed us up to find a balance and a joy in each other. This has not always been easy but was essential for our future.

Reflections from Kim

During the course of therapy, Alexia married. From the beginning Andrew was witness to Alexia's therapy from the outside. Now we began to think about how Andrew could become a part of our work together. DDP with families allows the therapist to help the parents, as attachment figures, to become witnesses to their children's unfolding stories, created with joint curiosity. As the parents respond with acceptance and empathy towards their children and these stories, the children come to experience themselves a little differently. New stories are jointly created. In working individually with Alexia, I missed having someone to witness. I wondered if it would be helpful to bring Andrew in to perform this role.

Alexia both wanted and feared bringing Andrew into sessions. Her fear, of course, was that he would not want her any more once he witnessed who she really was. Or worse, he would stay out of pity for her. She feared that involving Andrew would be the undoing of their relationship. I felt that Alexia needed to experience Andrew's acceptance of her, both to help her to find her own acceptance and as part of helping them to have a healthy relationship with each other.

I also recognised my need for an attachment figure to help me with the work of developing and deepening the affective-reflective dialogue that Alexia and I were developing, as in my DDP interventions with children. It was very tempting to bring Andrew in as a 'parent figure' for Alexia. This would have been a mistake. We already recognised the tendency that Andrew and Alexia had to be rescuer and victim. They needed help to move from this co-dependent relationship to a healthier relationship of reciprocity. We discussed this together, working out how Andrew could be supportive within the sessions, a witness to the story, whilst also encouraging them to work towards a more equal relationship of mutual support. I needed to keep in mind that they were attachment figures to each other, and bring Andrew into the work in a way that strengthened the reciprocity of this.

This posed me with another dilemma. Who was my client? Was my work with Alexia or should I also work with them as a couple? We had begun this work as individual therapy. It did not feel right to change this now. We decided to bring Andrew into the sessions as a witness, supporting Alexia in the therapy, whilst being careful not to ask him to be a parental figure. Alongside this they would work together on their relationship outside of therapy. We recognised that some couples therapy might be helpful for them in the future, but also felt that the work for Alexia needed to come first. This became even more evident when we came to work on the sexual abuse.

I met with Andrew separately initially. This was very brief; not the preparation I would do with a parent when working with a child. I wanted to keep the focus on Alexia as independent adult. I did however want to understand what issues from his own attachment history might be activated whilst witnessing Alexia's therapy sessions. This was important so that I did not ask him to respond at the wrong moment. It is important not to ask the witness to respond with acceptance and empathy at a time when they are feeling a lack of empathy. Their discomfort and defensiveness would lead to the client experiencing a lack of acceptance. This damages the trust and feeling of safety we have been building. For example, understanding that Andrew's history was one of emotional needs not being met, which had left him inclined to undervalue emotional experience, was helpful to avoid me asking him to respond to Alexia with acceptance when she was emotionally heightened. I needed to provide the co-regulation Alexia initially needed. As Alexia became more able to be reflective, then Andrew was able to respond to her. I also needed to coach Andrew in the attitude of PACE, recognising his tendency to reassure and helping him to return to the PACE attitude at these times.

Andrew responded well to my guidance, and his presence in the sessions he attended was really helpful. Alexia remained fearful of involving him whilst also recognising how helpful it was. She wanted him there but also feared his involvement. Her ambivalence was evident in that she would sometimes invite him into sessions and at other times would avoid this. We would discuss this together, always leaving the decision about when he should attend to her.

Watching Alexia with Andrew revealed her continuing difficulties with her sense of self and her fear of not being good enough. When he was there, she would be anxious and agitated. Most striking to me was her intense difficulty in looking at him. Her sense of shame in being known was very high. She also worried that she was asking too much of him, that this was selfish of her, wasting his time. Seeking help and support from Andrew was challenging her own need to take care of and please him. She was concerned that she would wear him out.

Watching Alexia with Andrew also revealed a very different Alexia to the one whom I had become used to during our sessions. Gone was the composure of the thoughtful adult who allowed me to support her in difficult exploration, accepting my co-regulation with ease. Instead I saw a frightened child who believed she would be exposed at any moment. This was life or death for their relationship. I began to appreciate how brave Alexia was in inviting Andrew into her sessions. In the therapy room there was no place to hide. Alexia truly believed she could lose everything. She also knew that without including Andrew their relationship would be built on a false foundation. She needed to experience his acceptance, even for the most shaming parts of herself. She had to trust that this acceptance would be there in order to go forward with the work. This was a leap of faith.

At the end of the session Alexia would grow back into her adult self. She could look at Andrew and chat to him again. She felt the closeness that his witnessing brought to their relationship. She could relax, knowing that he had witnessed her shame and was okay.

Her anxiety would build again following the session. Outside of the sessions, she continued to fear that she was asking too much of him; that she would wear him out, that she was not being fair asking him to do this for her. For now, within the sessions, she could have some respite from this pervasive anxiety. She could enjoy them being together, sharing the therapy experience. She could allow the intimacy that such sharing led to.

For me, having Andrew in the sessions was really helpful. I knew that we would be able to go further, more deeply, with his gentle witnessing presence. I used a combination of talking to Alexia, talking about her with Andrew and talking for her to Andrew to help us explore together. Talking to her was our familiar way of being. When this became too emotionally overwhelming, I could move to talking about her with Andrew. This moved the witness role. Alexia now became witness to our developing story as I described it to Andrew. This helped to calm her emotional arousal, allowing her to stay present and reflective. At times I sensed that Alexia could go emotionally deeper. Talking for her allowed this deepening. I would talk as if I was Alexia, putting her story into words. Again, Alexia was witness to her story but in a more emotionally involving way. She felt her story as well as observing it. Choosing which of these to engage in was my responsibility, guided by my relationship with Alexia; our intersubjective connection continued to guide me moment by moment.

Alexia recognised that having Andrew in these sessions allowed her to go to an emotionally deeper level. She appreciated having Andrew there to help her to do this, but this was always coupled with her ongoing fear that she would wear him out or contaminate him in some way. I encouraged them to take care of each other between sessions, aware that they were working out a new relationship with each other as a consequence of the work that Alexia was doing.

Over time Alexia and Andrew's relationship did change, helped I think by his involvement in the therapy. I noticed that Alexia became more attentive to Andrew's needs and less anxious about his availability to her. They discovered curiosity together about each of their stories, and joy in their relationship increased.

Chapter 10

FINDING COMPASSION – FROM SHAME TO PRIDE

FINDING ME

I learn to accept. Acceptance is the Achilles heel of the mask. Acceptance gets beneath the mask. It reveals who I am and can be.

Acceptance and compassion are hard. Sometimes it feels easier to be angry and fighting. Acceptance is my friend. With acceptance and compassion, I am stronger. I am wise. I am kind. I am courageous.

I notice how compassion fills me with warmth, starting in my stomach and filling the whole of me to the tips of my fingers and toes. With compassion I can move, and it also calms and grounds me. I feel unrockable. I am bouncy as I bubble with energy.

I struggle with responsibility. I am afraid I will fail. This is the legacy of having responsibility when so young. Now I am learning to be an infant, a toddler, a child. I am an adult discovering dependency for the first time.

I am a survivor, not a victim. I was so full of shame, but it was not mine to hold. I have let shame go. I am full of pride.

I talk with my husband. We explore new ways to be a couple. We are growing together. No longer victim and rescuer.

I find ordinary relationships around me, my dads, my husband. Maybe in time my siblings. I learn to expect less from my mothers.

I learn to be compassionate towards myself. I find my good enough nurturer as I learn not to seek for perfection. She stays close to me without getting too close. She is wise. She is gentle and soothing. Her melodic voice holds me, and I feel stronger because of her strength and confidence. She is confident in me, and in this journey that I am taking. Not hope. Hope carries the weight of expectations. She knows that things can change but does not weigh me down with a hope that feels conditional. I have known too much of that in my life.

I judge myself and feel anxious. This can get in the way of compassion. I learn to soothe the threat I experience. I learn to have compassion for the critical, hurt part of myself that continues to protect me even when I don't need it to. The part that looks for threat when no threat is there.

I am more aware of my body. I am surprised at what I notice. Yoga is helpful as I discover myself. I take care of myself and feel well. My compassionate self is full of warmth, flowing out of me. It doesn't deplete me but energises me. I am open and strong. I am playful. I can accept but also challenge. I have a balance within me. I am courageous. I feel pride when others notice this about me.

Some things remain difficult.

At last I understand that therapy will not fix me. This is an annoyance to me. I smile at the part of me that likes things to be sorted, wrapped up in a nice bow. I will always need to care for myself. I will always have less tolerance to stress than some other people. I will always be impacted upon by trauma. And that is okay. Therapy did not make all the difficult stuff go away. It helped me to live with my imperfect self in an imperfect world. I love being bouncy, but life has ups and downs and I find a balance that allows me to manage the rough as well as the smooth. My trauma made a path for me that was well trodden. Therapy has given me another well-trodden path. Where there was one, now there are two. I have choice and I have a flexibility that I did not have before.

I still find it hard to look at myself. I feel so anxious. It reminds me that I will always have times of feeling not good enough, not deserving. Compassion exercises direct me to focus on being well, happy and free from suffering. But these can be illusory. I can embrace these now, but life is also about being ill and unhappy, and about suffering. I learn to find compassion at these times too. Sometimes it is easier to think compassionate thoughts than feel compassionate feelings. I learn not to try too hard, to allow warmth towards myself to emerge when it is ready.

I feel pride. I have done so much. I have shown strength I did not know I had. I am caring. I am assertive. I have balance.

I don't want therapy to end. It has been a safe place for me. A place I can be me without any expectation of being different. I am reluctant to let it go. I am excited about the future, about what I can achieve and what I will do. I am a child on the verge of leaving home. I look back and feel sad about what I am leaving. Annoyed that growing up means leaving things behind. I am an adult ready to embrace my future.

The ground is firmer beneath me. My life was on a railway track going forward. I have found a track to the side. It was small but has got so much bigger. I have a different track ahead. I am discovering who I really am, and it is surprising. My fear does not hold me back any longer. I am excited to find out what else I will discover.

I am proud. I can talk about all I have experienced. I don't need to hide any more.

I am authentic.

Reflections from Alexia

I remember feeling really resistant to the compassionate work. I didn't do the exercises at home. I didn't even think about them. I didn't keep them in my mind. I felt cross towards the exercises, almost as though in acknowledging them I was losing Kim. I felt short-changed, it was the diluting of the relationship that the exercises represented. We needed to find a different way to do this.

It was so important therefore to do this work together. Home-work felt conditional. If I did it, it would be to please Kim. This would make the relationship conditional. I didn't do it. When we started to do the exercises together it felt totally different. When I am talking to Kim there is no right and wrong, I can say it as it is. It is more fluid. I feel more freedom to express myself. Kim helped me to access parts of me that I found hard to access by myself. I could have done this at home, but it would have stayed in my head. With Kim, I could access the feelings. Keeping the compassion work within the sessions felt like we were back on track.

This was also difficult because I couldn't see what compassion had to do with me. And yet I wanted to have a go, because Kim thought it was important and I trusted her. It felt like a parallel to when I wanted Kim to help me to become more perfect, but she would not collude with this. This was so challenging, but I learnt to trust her. I needed to do the same with the compassion work.

What was an easier part of this work was accessing others' compassion towards me. It felt impossible to find compassion for myself. It was like a wall – I could think it, I could know it, but the wall stopped me feeling it. This was really hard for me. We talked about this. We made sense of the wall. Compassion was like a seed that had never grown; the potential had always been there but the relationships around me had not allowed it to grow. There was an absence: I hadn't received compassion as a small child; I hadn't experienced any significant others modelling compassion towards themselves. I was surrounded by people full of self-criticism and harsh judgement.

Compassion was an alien world. The first time I noticed people being warm and compassionate towards themselves was during the time Kim and I were working together. It felt alien and it felt threatening. I didn't understand it. It made me question things – how can someone be so nice to themselves? How is this helpful to them? It felt like a Christmas advert, cosy and warm, but I was shut out in the corridor; I wasn't an invited guest. I noticed feeling angry towards these people. I was jealous; they had something I didn't have, and I didn't know how to find it for myself.

I started by imagining that I was someone else talking to me. I couldn't do it in my own voice yet; me to me was too hard. This was upsetting; why couldn't I do this? Why couldn't I just make it happen? I was like a toddler who couldn't get a jumper on. I felt so frustrated. Kim helped me to relax and to take the pressure off myself, trusting that it would come in time. And of course, it did. Without trying it spilled out of me; suddenly I was compassionate to myself. This was most clear when I was writing the compassionate letter. It felt amazing. I still can't believe I wrote those words to myself. Reading them makes me laugh and cry. I sound so authentic.

This letter brought therapy to a conclusion. I was a different person from the one who had started therapy. I now had a coherent sense of who I was; a sense of self based on authenticity rather than trying to please others. I am less afraid; the anxieties are still there but they are not controlling me any more. I can take risks; feeling angry, for example. I no longer have a sense of how dangerous this could be. I still fear losing others, but I now know this is less likely to happen and if it did it wouldn't break me. Before this it would have shattered me. It still doesn't feel safe to be angry, but I no longer feel this could kill me. The tigers are not stalking me any more.

It came as a shock to me that Kim thought I was ready to end. I was ready to manage the world by myself. This felt scary but also incredible that she had so much hope for me. She trusted that I had got this. I felt I was receiving a massive acknowledgment. Kim was saying to me that I could do this; I would find a way to manage whatever lay ahead.

Mmm, ending. What an annoying word. I didn't want this to end. I had never been so looked after. In truly wanting Kim's support I had shed unhealthy independence. Ending brought up for me that I was welcoming being dependent upon someone: something I had fled from all my life. I had found the roots to support my wings. I was ready to end, but it was also frightening. I had to trust that I could manage genuine independence. This meant standing on my own two feet and letting other people in to support me when I needed them.

I was helped in this because I now had an internalised voice coming from Kim. I could imagine her comfort and her suggestions when things were feeling tough. This is something I had never had before. I had moved around so much in my early childhood I had never had the opportunity to experience a clear voice that could guide me, just lots of conflicting echoes which left me unsure and alone.

Kim did offer me a safety blanket. She told me this was an ending for now. Within this there was an acceptance that life wasn't simple and that I might need more therapy in the future. I could come back when I needed to. In saying she thought it was time to end, she was letting me know it was okay not to be perfect. This did not need to be wrapped up in a bow, everything dealt with. Life would continue with all the challenges that were inevitably ahead. I trusted that I could ask for help again and that Kim would have space for me.

'For now' was important. It gave me a different experience of endings – it wasn't abandonment. It was less final than that. We were ending, not in a bad way. It wasn't my fault because I had worn her out. I was ready. This was the first positive ending that I had ever had. Not an ending that was about loss and abandonment, but an ending that was all about new beginnings. It was so important to have this ending. Kim had helped me to grow up and I was ready to 'leave home'.

Reflections from Kim

As we approached an ending to our work together, I felt that we needed a final phase. Alexia had grown through therapy from infant, to child, to adolescent, to adult. All these parts had been within her at the start. Each emerged in developmental order within therapy. I could sense a wholeness about her now as integration and healing had occurred.

I wanted something in the final sessions that would help to strengthen Alexia's resources. We anticipated that she would meet setbacks; times when she needed to revisit her story again. We predicted that her future would hold experiences within which she would again notice the impact of her early traumatic experience, becoming a mother being an obvious example. I wanted to help strengthen the integration and healing that Alexia had been doing, building her resilience for whatever lay ahead. Compassion-focused work lent itself to this task.

Initially I suggested that Alexia engage in some of the exercises suggested by this approach between sessions so that we could discuss them together. Alexia did try, but it soon became apparent that this was not what she needed. Her thinking felt incomplete compared to the rich discussions we had together. I had suggested activities for between sessions before. For example, I wondered if it would be helpful to write 'letters not for sending' to significant people in her life. There was no pressure on her to do this, just an invitation to try it if she thought it would be helpful. Whilst Alexia could see that it could be helpful, she found it difficult to do.

As we discussed her resistance to such activities and the compassion-focused exercises, we considered her dislike of 'homework', and her reluctance to put reflections into writing. As we thought about why these suggestions were not suiting her, the answer was obvious. It was not intersubjective, in the sense that we were not sharing the experience of completing these activities. DDP had been our guide throughout our work. The relationship between us was the containing structure that allowed the therapy to happen. We realised that we needed an intersubjective container, by working together, to facilitate this last piece of the work. We agreed that we would work on this in sessions, discussing and reflecting together as we always did, guided by the compassion-focused exercises. In this way we explored what compassion meant, discovered what Alexia wanted from a compassionate other and explored what her compassionate self looked like.

During this final phase of the work I experienced huge pride in Alexia and what she had accomplished. I had always known that she was courageous, with a resilience that she could draw upon. Alexia had used this courage and resilience to go on a therapeutic journey which involved much pain and struggling. She did this whilst also getting married, maintaining a job, and seeking a career. The progress she made was remarkable, and I was proud to witness this as we moved towards an ending.

This had been a long journey. We had worked together for three years. Therapy and recovery from trauma cannot be rushed. We needed time to build our relationship; for Alexia to trust me. We needed time for the telling of the story. We needed time to swim to the depths of the story. Understanding, processing, integrating and healing needs all this time. As I have written elsewhere,

'The longer-term nature of the counselling is essential to give client and therapist the time and space that they need to travel a long road together, allowing time for trust, safety, relationship, understanding and new narratives' (Golding & Gould 2019, p.118). As the last story I wrote for Alexia illustrates, our road was long and winding; a journey that Alexia took, with me along to support and guide. I wrote this story as a final gift at the end of the therapy. We have included it at the end of this book.

Alexia discovered who she was during the process of therapy. She had indeed found her authentic self and was surprised and delighted in some of the things she discovered. She looked happier and healthier. The Alexia who sat in front of me now was very different from the person who had started. It seemed to me that she had grown more comfortable in her own skin. She was also becoming much more compassionate towards herself, with acceptance for what she had been through and the impact this had had upon her development. Alexia could recognise her strengths and her vulnerabilities and was more at ease with both. This meant that she also recognised and dealt with reminders of her trauma more easily, so they were less triggering for her.

Alongside this I heard that Alexia's marital relationship was also developing. No longer victim and rescuer, they were discovering a mutually supportive relationship within which they each could be vulnerable and seek comfort from the other.

We carefully planned an ending to the work, determined not to avoid this. Alexia recognised a dislike of endings and would often end something prematurely. I recognised a desire to prolong work; it was hard for me to let go. I needed to reflect carefully about whether I was extending a piece of work because of my discomfort or in the interest of my clients. We therefore planned six sessions and discussed how to mark the ending in the final session. As Alexia does not like surprises, I warned her that I would give her a gift in our final session; what the gift would be I left hidden – a gentle challenge to her fear!

Despite this planning, the ending was coming up faster than we expected. When we had two sessions left, I realised that we did not have enough time to complete the compassion-focused work that we had agreed upon. Imagine two people, both recognising their own avoidance of endings, trying to decide what to do. We were both certain we wanted to end properly and were worried that extending our time together was a way of avoiding this! As we realised what was happening, we laughed together. We did not need to be rigid. We allowed ourselves the flexibility of an additional couple of sessions to complete this part of the work.

And still, this part of the work felt muddy and pressured. I think, on reflection, I planned too much. Ending with some compassion-focused work was helpful for Alexia to increase her resilience, but it meant we became governed by an agenda. This was unhelpful. The compassion exercises became central and the relationship slipped to the back. I was in danger of losing the DDP attitude that was at the centre of our work. It was better when we held the compassion exercises more loosely, allowing A-R dialogue to flow, responding with PACE and drawing on the exercises when it felt useful.

This was most evident in our penultimate session. I had the goal of helping Alexia write a compassionate letter to herself as our last session. This meant I wanted to do some work on developing Alexia's compassion towards herself. I tried to do too much without enough flexibility.

Trusting the process, instead of planning it, is the essence of what DDP is. When I had an agenda for the session, it felt pressured; the task became more important than our relationship. Once I allowed the plan to be held more flexibly, we saw how to adapt the exercises to suit Alexia. Instead of a pressure to finish the exercise, we had room for thinking together. We could jointly explore compassion and what it meant to us. For example, we discussed hope. My belief is that hope is compassionate, and important in order to make progress. For Alexia, hope represented pressure. Hope equated to other people having expectations of you. This echoed her fear of not being perfect; not being good enough. Alexia taught me to be careful that my hope is not experienced as lack of acceptance loaded with expectation that she will change. Discussing this helped us to find a shared language together. Hope took on a different, shared meaning for us; one that conveyed acceptance, allowing a way forward.

Pressures to be perfect echoed within both of us at the ending of the therapy. Alexia wanted to be fine; to have dealt with everything. A full stop, no revisiting. I wanted us to have done a complete piece of work. We had started this work to find authenticity, but we were both in danger of seeking perfection. We risked returning to Painted Doll rather than embracing the messiness that is being human. The messiness of our ending sessions was a reminder that to be human is to be imperfect. We did not need to extend therapy to find a perfect ending. I could trust that Alexia could take it from here. She would find help again when she needed to, but she had the compassion and the resilience to continue now without therapy.

We planned our last session. Follow-lead-follow had worked well for us, but I wanted something to provide a full stop to this piece of work. Here I took the lead, suggesting ending with compassionate letter writing. I held this plan loosely, happy to abandon it if it did not suit Alexia, but she liked the idea. Compassionate letter writing is described by Paul Gilbert (2009). I adapted a structure suggested at a workshop by Deborah Lee (Lee & James 2012). I also wanted this exercise to give us an opportunity to reflect on the work we were bringing to a close.

We did this together. We explored the letter that Alexia wanted to write to herself. I recorded this conversation. Later I would use the recording to turn the conversation into a compassionate letter addressed to herself. Alexia could then edit this letter, ensuring that it was personal to her; that it said what she intended. This collaboration worked well for Alexia. As might be expected, she began anxiously. She was concerned about whether she was being compassionate, exploring and judging her words as she spoke them. She worried about how to silence her critical voice. As we co-regulated these anxieties, she relaxed into her letter. Without the pressure to write and being able to reflect with me as we went along, Alexia could experience her own warmth and pride in what she had achieved. The intersubjective nature of this session led to two letters. In supporting Alexia to speak a letter to herself, we were both writing a letter to Alexia. These are included following this chapter. These letters provided the ending we had sought.

* * *

With the letters spoken we turn the recorder off. We sit together reflecting, as we have done so many times before. Louis Cozolino says:

> Having a conscious narrative of our experience helps us remember where we have come from, where we are, and where we are going. In other words, our stories ground us in the present, within the flow of our histories, and provide a direction for the future. (Cozolino 2016, p.241)

This is what Alexia had achieved through therapy. We will have one further meeting, along with Andrew: a celebration of what we have achieved. This, however, is our last therapy session. It is a time to look back as well as forward. A time to enjoy being in the present together.

For now, our work is done. A blackbird sings loudly outside. A song to accompany our reflections. This feels fitting as we reflect on the therapy whilst looking towards the future: a spring full of new beginnings as therapy comes to an end.

COMPASSIONATE LETTERS

Alexia's compassionate letter to herself

Dear Alexia,

A massive well done. I think you have surprised yourself that you got this far, but you have. Sometimes you forget how hard it's been. It's been a really long and difficult journey, but you still turned up and you did your best. I'd like to add that you didn't miss a single session. You can be a serial 'misser outer', so that's a really big commitment. That makes me really proud of you. It shows your commitment to making things better for yourself.

You haven't always been committed to taking care of yourself, but you are now. You are committed to taking care of yourself and having a healthy and fulfilling life. A life where you invite warm relationships and you give that back to people. That is something you never thought you would have, but you are having it. Even if you don't want to say it, you do have to admit that you've played a part in getting that. It feels awkward giving yourself credit, but some credit does have to be given. It's taken more strength than you ever realised.

As I talk to you, I can hear another voice that is trying to push this away, warning me off from being nice to you. I want to tell this voice to go away, but I also recognise that it has been keeping you safe. I like thinking about this voice as a superpower. Thank goodness this part of you was there; this small reptilian brain. I know what it was doing. It isn't a big part of you, but it is a very strong part. It is still looking out for threats. It is your clever spy that always knows before your head catches up. This is the bit that has kept you very, very safe in a very unsafe world. It is still keeping you safe, but to feel freer and happier and more fulfilled you need it to back off a little bit. It has done its job very, very well, and it has had to, but Alexia, you need a little bit of space now. You want to move forward. You need it to just take a step to the side so that you can keep moving forward and not feel stuck.

As I work on this letter at the end of therapy, I write to the Alexia who started. You can't see it now, but you don't have to be perfect. You are brave, and you will be brave enough to test this. Your flaws are what make you different, what make you unique. You worry that if people see them, they will banish you and they won't want you. I promise you that when you are brave enough to show those to people, they will care for you even more. They will accept you for all those flaws as well as all your strengths that you are so good at showing already. What you can't see at the minute is that true strength is allowing yourself to be vulnerable; allowing yourself to take jumps and leaps; to take risks. There is so much ahead of you at the beginning of this. You will get through a lot of tissues in the next three years and you will threaten to set fire to one of Kim's chairs! It will be that hard, but you will also like that you make Kim laugh; someone else gets your weird sense of humour.

Along the way you will meet many parts of yourself. You will meet Golden Doll. I'm not even going to call you the golden child, Alexia, because that isn't your name. This is the name you were given, and this was the expectation that people had for you. You worried that unless you lived up to this expectation you would be found out to be the worst person that nobody wants. The expectation can't be lived up to, by the way.

Actually, what you will go on to feel angry about is that you should never have been made to feel like you had to be a golden child. It is so far from who you are. You felt pressure to be amenable, polite, meet everyone's needs, remember the tiniest details about people to keep them happy, just to keep the status quo and to make people like you. That's not who you are and that's okay. It doesn't mean that you are a bad person even if you worry that it does. It doesn't mean that you are unlovable. It just means you are human. I'm not asking you to notice this now because it's a process. It is okay to worry, but there are things that don't fit with the golden child personality that you will like about yourself. For example, your assertiveness and how you are becoming quite direct and quite outspoken about the things you are passionate about. And you are a bit cheeky and push your luck a bit, and you were so afraid to show that part of you and it is a really good part of you. It is okay to feel like you have to be this way because right now that is how you feel you have to be, but you won't have to be this way forever, and you will find this out.

You were missed. Not that people didn't see enough of you, but you were overlooked. You shouldn't have been and that wasn't fair. You wished you were noticed way back and that is really sad and that is really unfair.

How you saw yourself and how others saw you were just worlds apart. You saw yourself as screaming out to be noticed, but it was a silent scream. You were so good at covering things, you had to be. People didn't see that, and you really wished they had. You wished that someone had gone: 'Is it really all fine? Let me understand that. Help me get that.'

You felt great pressure to be good all the time and not to ask for help. People relied on you being okay, being good and keeping others happy. People knew you for that. That was hard on you, very, very hard on you. In fact, it makes me wonder looking back how your brain didn't burst, or your heart. How you kept that together, I don't know. I am in awe of that I guess, because you couldn't do that now.

Before the golden child came into being there was an angry child. You will meet her too. Anger isn't bad, but somewhere along the line you found out, you were taught, that anger had no place in your life; it was dangerous, and it wouldn't be tolerated. Actually, that anger was so important and thank goodness it was there at some point. That anger was your way of saying that things weren't okay. You were still fighting to be noticed. You were still fighting for your needs to be met, and clever anger for doing that.

Other people just thought you were insolent, disobedient and manipulative. A child trying to be an adult and control other adults. That was your way of just expressing all the shit that was going on. That was your way of saying, 'Adults, you must notice. I don't understand what's going on, but it is not okay. Someone help me to understand that. People, notice me.'

I feel really sad that this angry child went. Actually, it didn't go; I think that is where your critical voice came from. I think you turned that anger on yourself and I guess that was the only way you could safely express it. Adults didn't notice and didn't keep you safe. It was too scary to be emotional or angry. That anger had to come out. Those feelings can't stay in. If anyone could have found a way to keep them in that would have been you, but you couldn't. I think that anger built inside. I think it ate away at you a bit. You took it out on your lovely skin, you hurt yourself. You held your breath and, with that, kept the anger locked up inside. It was the safest thing that you could do at the time and that is sad. You didn't deserve to feel like that about yourself. I wish you had someone to help you with that. I really wish that. You were so lonely. You have always felt lonely. I wonder if that anger was a way to get rid of that loneliness a bit. You were a locked-up book and you never let anyone else see what was inside.

Wow, you have come so far. You are much more open now, on your terms, with your boundaries. It makes me think about how amazed and proud I am of you. I forget that bit. I forget how far you have come. And some of that anger has come back out. It scares our husband and best friends sometimes!

And to truly understand why you buried the anger you needed to find the baby part of yourself. You were so angry with her at first. You don't feel like that any more. I'm sure you still worry that you are not good enough. That isn't going to go anywhere, but you do not see your baby part as demonic any more.

You want to say sorry for thinking that, but not in a way that you were wrong to think it. You were led to feel that way. This is what you were shown, what was communicated to you. You just feel a massive sense of loss. You should have had so much more. You shouldn't be learning about how to look after babies from a book now. You should know that intrinsically because that's what you should have had. You should have been rocked, sung to and taken care of. You should have been noticed and really loved, not because you could meet others' needs. Even decades later you still feel the loss of the mum that you wished you had; your mum being well and being the mum she could have been. That's so unfair. You didn't deserve that. These were the cards that you were dealt. It wasn't your fault. I wish you had had more.

I think you have come very far. You still worry that you are going to wake up from a dream. You feel a huge sense of guilt that your siblings are in such a different place at the minute. It's hard to recognise who you were. You mostly really like yourself now, and you never thought you would ever think or feel that.

You never believed that you would feel joy. It is different to what you expected. You didn't expect this was how joy would be. You feel it now, but you expected it to be very different. You thought you would be happy all the time. You thought you would be cracking jokes. You thought you would get better at jokes, which you definitely haven't! You always laugh at your own jokes.

Joy comes and goes. You thought you would switch it on when you wanted to, but joy is not like that. It's more real.

You don't join in people's laughter now unless you find it funny. People just laugh even when it isn't funny. You won't laugh. You would have done, used your most beautiful smile and laughed a lot, but you would have been completely blank behind the face. You would have no idea what was going on. If someone told you a joke, you would just laugh like your life depended on it. If you don't get it, you don't get it, you won't go along with laughter any more, unless you find it funny.

I think you were a victim and you don't see yourself like that any more. You felt such shame, and really that shame does not lie with you. It wasn't something you should have held; it was forced on you. That's where the victim thing comes in. It wasn't a choice. There has been a really big shift for you in losing the shame. You were done to. Even now you can become passive if you are stressed and feel under threat. The victim thing is really difficult, because you felt that was all you could be. You didn't think there was another option. You froze, it was all you could do at the time. Now there is assertiveness: 'No, I have some choice, I have some influence here.' If somebody makes a negative comment to you or changes the subject when you have something to say, automatically that would have been about you. You would have still felt shame. Now you can see that it may not be about you and you don't have to take it on. You have a choice about how you respond. It's the same with trauma. You are affected by it but there is some level of choice about that now. Not about being affected by it but how you manage it.

You are stronger than you know. I think you might be one of the strongest people I know. That's amazing. You are going to get by. Much as you would like to believe it's all up to the fates, you are a survivor. There is something in you that makes you want to do better and live a healthy life. There is something about you that makes you want to move upwards and onwards. I don't know where that came from, but it is there. You will worry. You will be your harshest critic, hard on yourself. That will be helpful in small ways because it keeps you grounded, but just remember to be kind to yourself as well.

And Alexia, you will be a good mum. You will be hard on yourself as a parent, a lot. It will be the most difficult thing that you have ever done, but you have so much love to give to your child. It is lovely that saying this makes you feel warm, and excited for the future.

As this therapy finishes it's really annoying to you that it isn't all sorted. That will always be an annoyance because you like things wrapped up in a nice bow. And I am smiling at the minute; it makes me feel warm towards you, because I like that about you, it amuses me. You needed to see that things weren't all wrapped up. This stuff leaves well-trodden paths. I think you needed to know that. But you've got another well-trodden path now too.

Love from,
Alexia

Kim's compassionate letter to Alexia

Dear Alexia,

We are coming to the end of this piece of work together. As I help you to write a compassionate letter to yourself, I find I too am writing a letter to you. Relationship has always been our guide during this therapy. We have chosen this last task to do together, and we do it relationally too. This feels right. As I put this letter onto paper, I think about the interlinking of our two letters, as we talk and reflect on the journey you have done. A journey which I have had the privilege to share with you.

I asked you to notice your courage, your resilience, your ability to cope. These have been so evident to me, from the very beginning, almost three years ago. I am so pleased that you can see these too. Initially you are self-conscious, feeling uncomfortable giving yourself credit. It is hard for you to notice that everything you have achieved has been down to you. You have a critical voice, warning you. You feel angry with it as it threatens the compassion you are trying to find. It is the voice of your hurt and fear. It is trying to protect you still. You want to tell it to go away, I help you to invite it in. In a way this is the most hurt part of yourself that is still trying to defend you. Take care of it, as it has tried to take care of you. As you do, you find your compassionate voice.

As you begin, you are preoccupied by the idea of a compassionate letter, anxious to get it right. You worry that you won't find warmth for yourself. As you continue, this anxiety drops away, the judging, critical voice quietens. Your compassion and your warmth towards yourself shine. I am so proud to witness this.

We think about the Alexia who arrived on my doorstep. You felt empty, false, you didn't feel authentic and you didn't want to be that person any more. It is hard to remember you as you were back then. You recognised who you were and who you wanted to be. You found me to help you become the person you wanted to be. The hard work was all yours.

I love the words you find to describe things, the analogies that let me glimpse into the world you had experienced. You talked about feeling like a painted doll in a painted doll's house. We opened the door to the doll's house and the first person we found was the golden child. How much you hated that term, a title that was given to you by others. You were other people's success story and it was a hard burden to bear.

I introduced you to acceptance, and didn't it make you grimace! You wanted to banish the golden child, but I urged you to embrace and care for her. Your first taste of how challenging therapy was going to be. Finding acceptance also means embracing the hurt and sadness. You were so brave allowing yourself to uncover a well of grief.

Finding the angry child led to sadness, but it was so good to watch you also finding your assertiveness. I could see you growing in front of me, I could see you becoming whole again. As a child you lost all sense of safety, you hid so much of yourself away. Therapy offered you safety to find those parts of yourself again.

As therapy progressed, we moved towards the hardest things of all. You were always so brave, taking every step you needed to. Often going towards it faster than I could imagine. Confronting the most vulnerable parts of yourself. Allowing yourself to feel the baby self again. And of course, having to face the abuse. I felt so sad as you thought you had finished and then we discovered that there was more to do. You always led the way. There were times you longed to be done with it, but you never faltered. Not one cancelled appointment in three years, that's pretty impressive.

I loved watching you becoming healthy in front of me: fewer headaches, more self-care. You described feeling bouncy, and I could see that in you. More importantly, you also allowed yourself compassion when it was harder, when you were more stressed and less well, when you needed to go 'offline' for a while. You were finding balance in your life.

There were plenty of tears, I always had the tissues ready, but we had laughter too. Joy was an important part of therapy, as well as in the rest of your life. You thought you could only find joy by getting rid of the 'difficult stuff', but you discovered joy in embracing this. You learnt early in life to find a smile. I know you practised in the mirror. It was a part of pleasing others, but it never reached your eyes. I witnessed you finding your authentic smile, as reciprocal relationships opened up to you.

Whilst you were a victim of developmental trauma, including sexual abuse, you came to me already a survivor. It was your will to survive that led you to seek out the help you needed. I am honoured that you chose me to seek this from. You survived and now you can thrive. I love how your future has opened up to you. I love how you have taken risks: marriage, work, friendships. You used every ounce of your resilience to go on this difficult journey. You had the courage to take the risks you needed to and the fortitude to deal with the ups and the downs. Along the way you found compassion and warmth for yourself.

We both would like things wrapped up, to find a perfect ending for therapy, but this would not be authentic. We are imperfect people in an imperfect world. That is what authenticity teaches us.

So Alexia, as this journey comes to an end, at least for the time being, you deserve a break. Go and find your future. You have many exciting adventures ahead of you: career, developing as a couple with Andrew and, I hope, motherhood. And when it is hard, as it will be, I know you will seek the support you need. This is what makes you a great wife, friend and one day a mother. It has been a privilege to help you find a new path and to ensure that it is as well trodden as the old one.

With love from your therapist, and friend,
Kim

AFTERWORD

Reflection from Kim

Ending therapy is such a significant moment. We wanted to mark it with the sharing of gifts; a small symbol of our work together and an acknowledgment that whilst our relationship as therapist and client was ending, we would each remain in the other's mind. This was especially important for Alexia, as being held in mind was something she had missed in her earliest experiences of relationships. We agreed we would each choose for the other a small memento of our work together. In addition, I chose to write a final story for Alexia.

Throughout the therapy I had written stories to capture the work we were doing at that moment. I now wanted a story to capture the whole. Therapy as a journey is an obvious metaphor, used many times, but that is how it felt. We had travelled together exploring the life experiences that Alexia had faced during her childhood and adolescence. We had moved together towards an adulthood within which Alexia could be authentic and whole. I chose to write the story of this journey, 'Beneath the Mask', and include it in full below. This built upon the first story of the

Russian Doll, which had a similar journey motif. Here the journey is brought to a point of completion. There are more journeys ahead, but this story marks the ending of this one. It was time to return home, where Alexia had a hopeful future waiting for her.

And so it continues...
A final reflection from Alexia

When I read the final story which follows, I felt warm. It was lovely. It made me cry but this did not carry the emotional intensity of the other stories. This story felt like a celebration. It also provided me with a summary of our work together. When I read the other stories, written within therapy, I was discovering things about me and my story. This final story felt more like reminiscence - hey old friend, I know you. All the parts were joining hands together.

As we finish writing this book, it feels important to acknowledge that I still have more work to do. This isn't the end of the story. Do stories ever end? I came to therapy with the intention of being fixed, all tied up in a bow. I discovered the impact of my experiences: they have left threads that are always going to be with me. There will be times when I will pick these threads up again and seek therapeutic support. Life is a kaleidoscope with beauty and flaws, both equally in need of appreciation.

Beneath the Mask:
A Therapeutic Journey

*This story is written for Alexia. In celebration of her
therapeutic journey which I had the privilege to join her on.*

She was nearly three decades in the making. Long years, full of loss, pain and disappointment. Full of dread that maybe it was her fault. Was she to blame for everything that had happened to her? There were calmer years, times of being cared for; but always there was a cost. She had to be good, golden even; giving to others whilst taking little for herself. And the anger, the rage, the need? All buried deep within her until she was rarely aware of them. Defence built upon defence protected her. It had formed a mask that she could hide behind. These defences had made her who she was today. But she felt false, painted wood, not flesh and bone. She was a kaleidoscope without its colours, her world was black and white. She could survive in a black and white world, but was this enough for her?

Recently she had become aware of a longing within her. She wanted to find herself, to see who she was beneath the mask. She wanted to grow, to feel real. She tried to please others, but it was false, a compulsion to keep her safe. This mask hid all that she was and could be. She wanted to reject who she had become, but she didn't yet know who she could be.

Longing was accompanied by fear. Could she find herself? Who would she find? And what would she lose in the process? She had a partner, friends, siblings, relatives. They all wanted her as she was. Would she still be acceptable to them? Would she still be the person they loved?

When longing was strong, she stepped onto new ground. But it felt unstable. Would this ground support her if she continued to walk forward? Fear was stronger; she stepped back to where it was safe and familiar. She might feel false, empty, but at least it was a self that she knew; a self that pleased others.

Her partner encouraged her. He offered her words of reassurance. He would be with her. He would always love her. He would not leave. She feared his words. He did not know the buried parts of herself. He couldn't know what he would find. How could he know that what was hidden would be acceptable to him? It felt too big a risk.

Longing and fear balancing each other. The scales tipping one way and then back again. Indecision paralysing her. She could not do this alone. If longing was to win, she needed a guide, someone to support her, encourage her, help her to find the way. There was someone, a memory from her childhood. She had been aware of this person, a benevolent presence in the background. Someone who was interested in her and helped others to think about her. Could this be the guide she sought? Could this be the person to give her the courage to seek what she needed? She called and the guide responded.

They talked together exploring what could be. She felt no pressure, only encouragement. She didn't need to do this alone. The guide offered her an acceptance that she could not find for herself. This gave her hope that whatever happened, this one person would stay with her. It was an acceptance that frightened her. She liked it, wanted it, needed it. Someone who would be there for her no matter what. But would she? Like her partner, the guide did not know the buried parts of herself. Did not know all that she had been, all that she had done. When she knew, how could she accept? What if the guide helped her to reveal the real her and didn't like what she found? Was this another risk that was too big to take? The guide's quiet presence offered her some comfort. Could she risk losing this?

They talked back and forth for many days. They explored fear together. They embraced longing, and eventually this won. She was ready to begin this journey. She would set out to discover who she was. She did not know the way. She did not know how long the journey would last. She would leave behind a life that was safe and comfortable, perfect in many ways, but utterly, utterly false. However messy, she was finally ready to discover a life that was real in its imperfections. Whatever she found, at least it would be authentic; the rest she would figure out as she travelled. She drew strength knowing that her guide and her partner would be on this journey with her. For now, that was enough.

She opened the gate and took tentative steps forward. This time she didn't retreat. Partner on one side, guide on the other. She was not alone but, in many ways, this was the loneliest she had ever been. This search to find herself might result in her losing everyone in the process, but she had begun.

The valley

It was early in the morning when she walked away from her house and garden; the path stretched out before her. The gravel beneath her feet felt good, letting her know the journey had begun. The sun was already up, and it was warm on her face. She was on a country lane paved by trees. Crickets chirped and the birds were alive with song and the busy-ness that spring brings. She could hear the call of a buzzard circling high above her. As she walked, she took sips from her water bottle. She felt no rush. She could walk as fast or as slowly as she wanted to. This was her journey, and she could set the pace. She felt completely safe here and knew that this was a good place to begin. She did not know what was ahead, but she drew confidence from knowing that this safe place would always be there waiting for her. She wanted to get on, to find out what was ahead. She might discover parts of herself that she did not like, and did not want, but at least she would know who she was.

It was lunchtime before the path changed. As she left the lane the trees thinned, and the path broadened. She could glimpse a valley ahead. The wind was increasing; a wind that matched her mood, at first tentative but gradually getting stronger. Her muscles were already aching from the unaccustomed exercise. She sat on a nearby tree stump and ate the sandwiches she had brought with her. She did not take long. Now she had started she was eager to make progress and the valley beckoned to her. If she kept up a good pace, maybe she would reach it by nightfall.

The sun was setting, and the valley was bathed in red light.

It was time to stop for the night. Exploration would wait for the next day. She looked around and found a shelter that would protect her whilst she slept. Food was laid out for her. She could not see her guide, but her nurturing presence was all around. She ate and then crawled into the sleeping bag. Sleep was hard. She tossed and turned for much of the night. Her mind was restless, troubled. When she did sleep her dreams were full of images that she could not quite remember once she woke. It left her with a feeling of disquiet. Finally, as dawn broke, she got up and bathed in a nearby stream.

The weather again matched her mood as she set out to cross the valley. The wind gusted and then quieted. The sun poked out from behind a cloud and then scuttled behind another one. As she walked, she fell into a rhythm which soothed her. The weather calmed as well, and a light breeze and gentle sunshine settled around her. She thought she would cross the valley by the quickest route, anxious to make progress. The valley had other ideas. She walked along the straightest path only to find it circling in on itself. Whichever way she went she just moved deeper into the valley. This troubled her. She wanted to move forward, to get this journey over with, but the valley seemed just as determined to slow her down.

She sat down, resting whilst she decided what to do. Her guide came and sat with her.

'This is the valley of your defences,' her guide told her. 'You cannot pass through until you have acknowledged these.'

'Why would I want to do that?' she queried. 'I want to get rid of my defences. They are the reason I am who I am, empty and false. Surely I need to get away from them?'

'They have made you who you are,' the guide answered. 'But don't be too ready to turn your back on them. They have made you strong enough to survive, to thrive even, despite everything you have endured. Honour your defences, allow them to stay a part of yourself. Finding you does not mean losing who you have been.

These defences can still be helpful to you. Accept them and they won't need to be in charge any more. Work with them and become who you were meant to be.'

She had a lot to think about. This journey was going to take longer and be harder than she had imagined. She wanted to be a snake shedding its skin, losing the parts of herself that she didn't like. If she couldn't do this, what was the alternative? How could she accept these parts of herself without losing something as well? How could she honour her defences when she didn't even know what they looked like?

'Don't worry about that,' her guide smiled. 'They will find you.'

Defence one

She carried on walking, feeling calmer. The way became easier now she had stopped fighting the path. She fell into a rhythm again, resigned to whatever lay ahead.

It was late afternoon when she first felt a change. It wasn't just the temperature dropping. She felt someone or something watching her. She slowed her pace and looked around. Nothing.

'Look again,' a voice whispered in her ear. She looked in the direction it had come from. Slowly a pattern emerged out of the background of leaf and bark. An animal took shape. It was balanced on the bark of a tree, its long tail stretched behind.

'Oh, you are beautiful,' she said, but in the blink of an eye it had gone. 'Where are you?' she called.

'I am here, but I am *not* beautiful. You don't see me if you think that!'

She was startled. This was so close to how she felt. She often wanted to hide too, but this animal had got it to perfection. 'Come back,' she called. 'Let me see you. I won't make any judgement.' Slowly the chameleon reappeared. It had moved along the branch where it was greener, and its colours blended perfectly.

They walked together for the rest of the day. They had much in common and fell into relaxed companionship. It was like finding part of herself. The guide laughed at her for thinking this. 'She is part of you! She represents one of your defensive layers. Can you figure out which one?'

'The chameleon changes its colours to blend in,' she mused. 'I can recognise that. Not wanting to be noticed, but I think there is more. It feels like a part of me that wants to please; to take care of others whilst not being noticed myself.'

The chameleon agreed. 'Yes, and it is such hard work! I wear my colours like a mask. I hide behind them. I am attentive to what others need but I make no demands myself.'

Together they explored the burden of pleasing: taking care of others whilst having no-one to look after them. The strive to be perfect for fear of being lost. 'I'm tired of being the grown-up,' they both agreed, as they reflected on the childhood they had sacrificed along the way. They had responsibility so early it left them afraid. They feared failure in all that they did.

'And what happens to all those needs that a small child inevitably has?' she wondered. They thought about this. The chameleon thought about the effort of always blending in. 'We have to hide so much of ourselves; they are the unacceptable parts that we don't what others to see.'

'Yes,' she agreed. 'There is no place for our needs. It is these that make us unacceptable to others. They must be hidden from view. And what do we need?' she asked with a small voice. She was almost afraid to ask the question. She sensed the answer would be difficult, knowing the chameleon represented something that would be woken within her if she accepted it.

'That's easy,' said the chameleon. 'I want to be loved. I want to be noticed. I want others to want me for who I am, not for what I can do.'

As the chameleon spoke, she felt a pain in her chest. This echoed so much of what she felt. This was a part of her that she had lived with for so long, ignoring her needs in order to be acceptable to others. Trying to please, trying to be good, trying to be perfect enough that she would never be found out. This is what she feared; that others would realise that she wasn't what she pretended to be. It was exhausting trying to always be what others wanted. The chameleon expressed this so clearly.

'What do I do now?' she asked her guide.

'Embrace this part of yourself,' the guide responded. 'It is the part of you that is kind and caring. But listen to the chameleon and discover what you need. Let others take care of you too. You will experience more balance this way.'

'But what if others don't want to take care of me? What if I become too needy and they pull away from me? How do I find the balance between caring and being cared for?'

'You will need to take some risks. Test out different parts of yourself. Sometimes you might be too needy. This is all part of finding out who you are. Let others in and you will find your balance.'

Her partner whispered to her, 'It's okay, I'm here too. This is something we can do together.'

She smiled. Yes, it felt good to know she didn't always have to please others. There was room for pleasing herself too. The chameleon wrapped itself around her. She breathed a sigh of relief as they merged together. The chameleon's colours made her world a little less black and white.

She spent time resting after this. Days, weeks, months? Time seemed to lose meaning within the valley. She allowed herself to be looked after. She felt needy and it frightened her, but it was also okay. She knew there would be those in her life who would struggle with the new self that was emerging. In finding herself, she knew she risked losing others. But it also felt freeing. She would still be kind and caring, but she would remain aware of what she needed. It surprised her to find that she felt strong. She had always thought need was a weakness, now she discovered it was a strength. It saddened her that others had not found this acceptable when she was a child. The actions of others had taught her to bury this within herself. She had sacrificed a lot to keep others close. Whilst it was scary to allow this to emerge now, it also felt right. She was ready to continue with her journey.

Defence two

As she continued walking deeper into the valley, the landscape became more rugged. Trees were replaced by mountains and rock. She rested in natural caves when tired, but otherwise set a good pace. Occasionally she heard a distant roar. This made her hesitate, but her guide whispered to her, encouraging her to keep going. Once she saw a flash of red in the distance. She didn't recognise it, but the sights and sounds ahead filled her with dread.

At last she came to a plain leading to the foot of the largest mountain. She was not sure which way to go. Should she navigate around the mountain? Its size alone suggested this would be a long trek. She stood looking at the mountain rising before her. The dark rock at the base gave way to sunlit snow as she looked upwards. The summit was bathed in shadow; a broad, narrow peak. She had no mountaineering experience. She couldn't climb this. She would cross the plain. She hoped a way forward would emerge once she got closer.

Night-time was approaching as she neared the mountain. A decision about how to proceed would have to wait. Now her priority was shelter and food. She looked for a cave or shelter within walking distance. She was aware that the crows were circling nearby, a familiar and more comforting sound than the noise she had heard earlier. She watched them and it was as if they called to her: 'Come this way.' She guessed that this was just a trick of her ears, but she went anyway. Much to her surprise it led to the mouth of a cave. Hopefully, she ran towards it and got inside just as darkness descended.

It took her a while to become accustomed to the darkness, but when she did, she realised that the cave led to a tunnel sloping gently upwards. Again, she felt the dread she had experienced earlier. She did not want to go through the tunnel. She turned her back on it and looked for somewhere to rest. As she searched, she found a small chamber to the side. It contained food and blankets. She was in the right place. She would sleep here tonight and worry about the tunnel in the morning.

She slept fitfully, her dreams full of ominous noises and threats. In the morning her guide came to her. 'Today you will face your second defence,' she told her, 'but you will not be alone. We will do this together.'

She understood that the tunnel was her way forward. Without taking this route she could not leave this valley. The tunnel would lead her through to the other side of the mountain. But what would she have to face along the way? She did not feel at all brave, but the presence of the guide was comforting. She wouldn't hesitate any longer. She might not feel brave, but she was courageous!

The tunnel stretched upwards for hours before it started to level out. As she walked along, an unfamiliar but pungent smell became stronger and stronger. Everything was eerily quiet, but a presence could be felt everywhere, full of anger and menace. Every part of her told her to turn and leave. Put this danger behind her. Nevertheless, she kept on going, one foot in front of the other, taking her forwards.

And then, with a roar, it was upon her. Rearing up in all its magnificence and anger. 'Go away,' it seemed to be saying. 'Get out of my space.'

She knew that sentiment well. She had used her own anger to keep people away often enough.

She held her ground, looked the dragon in the eye and waited. It appeared discomfited. It roared again and breathed out fire. She almost laughed. Really, a dragon breathing fire! Again, she stood her ground, the guide giving her confidence. The flames did not hurt her. Instead she felt an answering anger rise within her. Not her usual burst of anger, quickly suppressed. This was a sustained feeling of intense rage that she hadn't felt for many years. She remembered feeling like this as a small child; her rage pushing people away, getting her into trouble. She was the problem child. She remembered learning to control it. It became a simmering white heat within her. And then she pushed it even further away. She got rid of the anger so that she could become what others wanted her to be. What had happened to her in the process? What had happened to her anger?

'You are my anger,' she said to the dragon. 'The roaring, the flames, they are a part of me. I haven't allowed myself to be angry for so long. I don't think I want it back. It just brought me a pile of trouble. I feared that I would hurt someone. My anger felt so big I thought it might kill. I had to make it go away. My anger could have led to me losing everything.'

'But how can you be you if you deny this part of yourself?' the dragon replied. 'Without me you will be empty.'

'It was dangerous to feel angry,' she retorted. 'No-one came to help me. I was all alone. I had to lose my anger to be taken care of.'

'That was then, and this is now,' the dragon challenged. 'Maybe it will be different now.'

'How can anger be okay? It makes me feel such a bad person having this anger within me. If I show it, everyone will know this about me.'

'That is what you were taught. Instead of recognising your distress they just saw your anger. They didn't understand that anger is neither right nor wrong, it is just an expression of what you are feeling. You were so little, and without help you could not find a way to show your anger safely. That is why you buried it. I have lived within the mountain ever since.'

She still wasn't sure, but as the dragon spoke to her the anger felt less scary. Could she welcome this part of herself back? The dragon watched her hopefully. He had been alone for so long. Above everything he wanted to be free. Free to feel angry. Free to express this safely and be accepted for it.

'Take me with you,' the dragon pleaded. 'You will be able to manage it. I will be there to help you. Together we will figure out how to be angry safely. Trust me, we will find a way. Just think how it will feel to be assertive, to be able to stand up for yourself. You are seeking balance within you. This will help.'

And so, she agreed. She welcomed the dragon in. Together they made their way out of the mountain and to the other side of the valley. They spent a long time together, getting used to each other again. Sometimes she could feel huge rage within her. It felt like fire. She was almost afraid to breathe! She needed to get used to these feelings again; to manage them. Her guide and her partner were there, encouraging her. She was soothed by their acceptance. They did not fear her, no matter what anger she displayed. Even when it emerged unpredictably, they were there taking care of her.

The dragon became a part of her, and she felt stronger. She was more assertive, a strength she didn't know she had. No longer would she just do what others wanted, what felt safest. She would make her own decisions, go where she wanted to go. She was becoming her own person.

'I see you have more colours,' noticed her guide. It was time to move on.

Defence three

She moved on through the valley and the landscape changed again. The trees were smaller, and tamer. There were open spaces, and saplings were growing to fill them. Small streams flowed through the woodland. It all had a sense of newness and growth. A relief after the mountainous terrain that she had been in.

She enjoyed this part of the journey. It felt invigorating. She wondered what was ahead for her. Who would she meet in this gentle woodland? She felt some confidence that she would be able to deal with whatever she found.

Nothing could have prepared her for what was to come. The challenge she was about to face. This gentle land held the hardest part of her defences. The changeability of the chameleon and the need it awoke within her, the fierceness of the dragon and the anger it filled her with, were nothing compared to the vulnerability she was about to face.

She found it in the most innocent of forms. She was walking along the side of a bubbling brook when she heard a noise. It was small and pitiful. She bent down and saw a tiny creature, immature, alone, defenceless. Her first instinct was to run. She wanted to leave this small and needy thing behind her.

The guide gently steadied her. 'Stay and take care of it,' she advised.

She could feel anger rising inside herself. Anger at its vulnerability. 'No,' she shouted. 'It disgusts me. Why should I look after it? It is a demon. If it wasn't for it, our mother would have cared for us. If it hadn't been so small, and so weak, we would have been alright.'

She was surprised at the strength of feeling this tiny creature evoked in her. She was comfortable with vulnerability in others. The little baby in the village, for example, never gave her these strong feelings of contempt and dislike. She understood his need, whilst envying the care he received. This was different. It was part of herself, and she hated it. If it had not needed so much, she would have been fine. She would leave this part of herself behind. 'I cannot accept this,' she told the guide. 'How can I be strong if I'm so vulnerable?'

The guide looked at her with gentle eyes. 'This is so hard for you. How to accept the parts of yourself that make you vulnerable. It is understandable when your youngest self was not cared for. You think of strong and vulnerable as opposites, but it is only with vulnerability that you will be able to grow emotionally. Your strength develops out of your vulnerability.'

Horror rose within her. She wanted to resist this with everything she had. She walked away. This was too hard. How could she accept this challenge? Weakness had always been her downfall. It was when she was at her weakest that she had felt most lost. This was the need that had to be buried the deepest. To survive neglect and abuse she had to be strong. Anger had helped her first, and then her self-reliance. This was what had led to the mask. Her defences grew out of denying her vulnerability, and then her anger. The mask helped her to become what others wanted her to be. Only then did she feel safe. Now this journey was asking too much of her. To go back, to retrieve the neediest parts of herself. To accept that they lived within her still. She thought about all she had accepted on this journey and knew that this was the hardest of all.

Her guide accepted these parts of her so easily, and this was almost her undoing. To feel care and love towards the smallest, youngest parts of herself. It felt as if it was cracking her completely open, exposing the worst of her. Acceptance weakened the mask. If she allowed this acceptance, the mask would drop. What would everyone see? What would be left? Would she be revealed in all that was bad about herself?

She agonised about this for many weeks. The guide stayed with her, patient and kind. Never pushing her. Accepting her fear, her distrust, her inability to do what she needed to do.

Gradually and bit by bit, the guide's acceptance reached her. She found it harder to resist the need within her. To avoid feeling vulnerable and exposed. She was kind and caring, able to look after others when they needed her. Why not look after the little joey as well? For this was what represented the youngest parts of her: a small joey, lost, unable to return to the kangaroo pouch it needed to grow and thrive.

If this was a part of her, it raised other questions. Was she worth taking care of? Maybe when it all went wrong it was her fault. If she had been stronger, not needing so much, would she have been loved and cared for? If she accepted the joey now, would it reveal her badness to all? Was this the loss she most feared: being found out as not good enough? Will everyone she cared about turn their backs on her? She needed to be strong. She needed her self-reliance. These protected her from losing what she needed most.

The guide reminded her that her defences were her heroes.

They had kept her safe for many years. In accepting herself, the whole of herself, she can also accept her defences. There will always be times when she needs to be self-reliant, compliant or angry; even times when it is helpful to hide her neediness away. In becoming whole, she will use these flexibly rather than be governed by them. She won't need the mask any more. She can be her genuine, authentic self.

She heard the words and they did make sense, but her heart felt different. She looked at the joey again but only felt anger towards it still.

'Why did you have to be so weak?' she asked it. 'Why did you make it so dangerous for us? Without you I would have been strong. I wouldn't have needed anyone. I would have been safe.'

'Without me,' responded the joey, 'you wouldn't have grown. It all started with my immaturity, my vulnerability. You could only grow emotionally from this start. You have denied this all your life, but you can't deny the truth. You have grown, but in many ways you are still a small, vulnerable infant trying to survive in the world alone.

'I always longed to be taken care of, to feel my mother's arms holding me safe. I believed it was because of you that I didn't have this. You were unacceptable to my mother and so I had to deny you. If I could have been what she wanted I would have got what I needed. If I accept you now it feels like I will be giving up on my dream for a mother's love.'

She walked by herself, thinking of everything said and unsaid. Acceptance and distrust battled within her. She needed this time alone. She needed to find a balancing point again.

Her need to be alone was respected. Her guide and her partner continued to take care of her whilst allowing her this time to work it out. She found this care in the resting places she needed, in the food that sustained her physically. She was being cared for and it felt kind, and good. Emotional nurture too was contained within these gifts of warmth, shelter and space. She had longed for this all her life, but she still feared losing everything. If she became whole, would she also be found wanting? If she became whole, would she lose what she was beginning to appreciate so much? This felt like such a big risk. If she reached for what she needed, would she wear others out? There were only so many tears that someone could deal with. What if she fell apart and no-one was able to help her come together again?

One morning she awoke and found resolution in her heart. It would take every ounce of her courage, but she would do it. She knew there was much within her that needed to be expressed. She had feared that these were the bad, contaminated parts of herself. She wanted to get rid of these. Now she realised that acceptance was not tolerating the unacceptable. It was understanding, without judgement, all that she felt. 'It is as it is,' she thought as she resolved to accept these parts of herself.

The sun shone brightly as she returned to the brook and the little joey. Gently she picked it up and cradled it in her arms. She spoke softly now, no longer blaming, but accepting these vulnerable parts of herself. The joey burrowed into her, accepting the warmth it had needed for so long.

She rose then, finding it strange to once more know these first parts of herself. They had been hidden for so long. She felt both stronger and weaker as she allowed this part the space it needed. A huge sadness engulfed her. Sadness for the tiny self she had been, and for denying this part for so long.

Her journey had not reached an end, but she allowed herself some time in this gentle part of the valley to rest and recoup. Her way ahead was clear; she could see the path leading out of the valley. She would rest. She would give herself time to grow used to herself. She would let herself absorb the colours she had found within the valley. Her kaleidoscope allowed her to look at the world differently, no longer black and white but full of colours. This brought its own complexity. A world less simple but more hopeful.

The waterfall

She left on a cold, crisp day. Snow had fallen overnight and it lay fresh and seductive before her. What looked soft and inviting was also cold and cruel. The next part of her journey lay ahead of her.

Walking through the snow was exhausting. With each step it tried to hold on to her, as if trying to stop her progress. Sometimes she lost the path altogether and she fell into the snowdrifts. She struggled on, each slow step taking her towards something. She was not sure what she was going to find but she noticed a growing ache within her, matching the physical ache from walking.

At last the snow thinned and the path became easier. She could hear a roaring sound ahead. Not the roaring of the dragon this time; it was the sound of water falling. As she walked it grew louder. Soon it was all that she could hear.

The waterfall filled her senses. As she allowed herself to become lost in its sensations, she noticed a deep longing. The waterfall fell in an endless stream of water, always falling but never staying. She wanted someone to stay with her, to hold her and make her feel the most special person in the world. She wanted unconditional love. She wanted a mother. Like the waterfall, it seemed within her grasp but then it flowed away.

She understood that her own mother had found life difficult, but the impact on her was hard to bear. She had never felt good enough for her mother and therefore did not understand that she deserved love and protection. The absence of unconditional love had left a hole she had been trying to fill ever since.

She was held in the waterfall's hypnotic grasp, unable to leave. Held by a dream which remained unfulfilled. She could not leave, it felt too much like abandoning this dream. If she moved away, a possibility would be lost forever. She had feared dependency for so long, now it seemed it was all she wanted. Her grief spilled over; her tears joined the ever-flowing water. She cried until she was spent, and then sat emotionally exhausted.

Her partner came to her. He took her in his arms. 'I am here. I will love you.'

'You are not a mother,' she replied. She was right. She was loved and she loved in return. They each cared for each other and that was as it should be. She was grateful for her partner's love. But she grieved for the mother that she would never have. The knowledge that this would not be hers was hard to bear.

This was an intense time. She experienced emotions that she had buried for many years. She had resisted this grief for so long, fearing it would be too much for her. Now she was surprised to find herself feeling lighter, as if a burden was lifting from her. She knew she would always have this sadness, but she felt that she could move forward again. She would be alright.

Finally, she could leave the waterfall. She would always regret what she hadn't had, but she did not need to cling to her desire any longer.

She felt ready to go home, renewed and reborn. She was stronger, lighter and more vulnerable. She felt more balance than when she had started this journey. She had grown emotionally even whilst she was accepting the younger, more immature parts of herself. She was adult, adolescent, child, toddler and infant. She was whole.

She set out on the path in front of her confident it would lead to home and her journey's end. How wrong she was!

In the jungle

Several weeks passed. She settled into a rhythm of walking and resting. Her sleep was troubled, haunted by dreams. In the dream she was being hunted. She tried to evade the creature, but it always caught her. Then she would wake up. She did not know what this meant, and it troubled her.

She asked her guide, who questioned her closely. 'How do you feel,' she asked, 'whilst you are being hunted?'

'Scared, obviously,' she reflected. 'I believe it will hurt me, kill me even, if it captures me.' She thought hard. Her memory of the feeling of terror was palpable, but there was something else. Something underneath the terror. 'Humiliation,' she said. 'That is what I am feeling. The animal is playing with me, nearly catching me and then letting me go. I just feel humiliated. I am a victim to its power and control. I am powerless. It intrudes on me in every way possible, so big and strong, standing over me. I can do nothing but let it do what it wants even though I know that this is contaminating me. I can't run, I can't fight. I am just left frozen in its grasp.'

'Ah,' said her guide. 'There is a part of your experience that you haven't confronted yet. I fear this is going to be hard for you. You will have to confront things that you have tried hard to forget.'

She was dismayed. She thought she had faced everything and now there was more! She had an intimation of what this was about, and it horrified her. 'I thought I was done. I don't want any more,' she cried.

'I know,' said the guide. 'This feels so cruel. You have come so far, faced so much. Now you have more to face, and these memories will be the hardest of all. Things you have never told anyone, but memories that you need to share. You are more whole than when you started, but there are still some cracks we need to attend to.'

She thought about what the guide had said. Yes, it was true. Her partner knew much of what she had experienced but there were things she hadn't even told him. She could feel the impact on their relationship. He held her hand. 'We will face it together,' he said.

'I am a broken vessel; a cracked pot that can never be whole again,' she told him. 'I don't think you will want me when you see all the cracks.'

He smiled at her. 'That is a risk we have to take.'

And so, they entered the next part of the journey together, the guide silently by their side. They entered a jungle. They could feel the humidity rising as they moved along the path. The foliage was a vibrant green, verdant and lush. The trees rose high above her. She could hear wildlife all around. A cacophony of insects and birds. She glimpsed monkeys high up in the canopy, chattering to each other as they jumped from tree to tree, the creepers giving assistance as needed.

But always she felt a menacing presence. It appeared to be all around her. Just as in her dreams, she knew she was being hunted. Her instinct was to run and hide. Initially she followed her instinct, but all this did was leave her lost and lonely. Inevitably he would find her, and she felt more lost than ever. He played with her, this ever-present predator, allowing her to hide for a while and then finding her again.

Gradually he took shape. She saw a tiger, glorious to behold, but more corrupt than any real tiger. His motive appeared benign but there was a hidden menace.

Now he spoke. He told her of his love for her, how special she was to him. She wanted to believe him, but she felt revolted. She would bathe in the river, trying to wash away the contamination she felt.

Running and hiding was not working. She just grew more lost. She changed tack. She tried to please him instead; to placate him in order to keep herself safe. She offered food; she tolerated his games. She felt wicked to her core. She felt truly evil treating him this way.

One night the guide lit a fire and sat with her. The fire warmed them and kept the tiger away. 'It is time to be free of him,' she said. 'Tell me your story.'

'I'm afraid,' she replied. 'Will you still be here when I am finished? I fear this will be my undoing. How can you accept me still when you know what I have done?'

'I will be here,' the guide said.

And then she told her story. A very young child, in a village that could not protect her and a man who wanted more than a young child should have to give. She did what she could to protect herself. She avoided him when she could. She tolerated his 'games' when she could not avoid him. Always she felt a menace behind his smiles. She feared for her life.

The guide listened. She did not leave. She held her through the telling. It took several weeks before the story was told. After each telling she needed to rest, to gather her strength for more. Then her partner's arms would be there to comfort her.

Finally, it was done. Along the way she found compassion for the small child who was so badly hurt. She discovered admiration for the teenager who freed herself from the danger and continued to live her life. She found understanding for the forgetting of this story, and relief for the remembering. She was free of it at last.

She was no longer a broken vessel but was made strong and beautiful in the mending. Now she could confront her biggest fear, facing feelings that she had held within her for so long in order to show the tiger that she was no longer afraid of him. She left the shelter and went out alone. She knew she would not have to wait for long. He came, of course, ready to hunt and pursue, ready to take her gifts. What he didn't expect was to see her steady, ready to face him. She stepped forward. She didn't run. She didn't placate. She shouted all the rage she felt at how he had treated her. She shouted until her anger was spent. He stood there, absorbing it all. No tiger now, he would hunt her no more. He gave her one more look and then turned and walked away.

She felt freer than she had ever done before. Now she could leave the jungle; her task was complete. She no longer believed she was bad, but a victim of badness. She had survived and at last could go home.

Her journey was complete, at least for now. 'Our stories always need revisiting,' her guide told her, 'as our life progresses, but I think this will be the most painful revisiting you will do.'

Going home

She found the path to home and followed it with determination. As she walked, she reflected on all she had encountered and how different she felt. Stronger, lighter, balanced and authentic. She understood herself more fully now. She had wanted to lose parts of herself but had found compassion for these parts instead. She could be honest and true to herself. Not perfect, but not bad either. She had human frailties, of course, but also the courage to face the world and to be seen.

At last she arrived home, back to the place where she had started. It looked different somehow, or maybe she was looking at it with new eyes. It was the same house, the same garden, but less perfect. No longer a painted home for a painted, empty lady but a real home for a real person made of flesh and bone.

Her partner was with her. He held her tight as they walked into their home.

'You have cared for me so much during this journey. I am so grateful to you,' she told him. 'A part of me can't quite believe you are still here after all you have discovered about me. You have never flinched. I have accepted so much about myself. I couldn't have done this without your acceptance first.'

He smiled at her. 'It has been a privilege. You are so brave, so courageous. You have done the hard work. If my being with you made it a little easier, then I am pleased.'

'And what now?' she said. 'I am not the person who set out. I worried in finding myself I would lose you, but you are still here. How will our relationship grow now?'

'We will find that out together,' he reflected thoughtfully. 'We still have work to do as a couple and that does make me fear. What if I can't make the changes needed of me? What if there are difficulties in our relationship that we haven't realised? I am not sure I have your courage. Caring for you has been easier because I have not had to look at myself. I am not as good at facing things as you are. I find it easier to ignore things, hoping they will go away.'

She took him in her arms. 'I am here for you. We will be stronger as a couple now, each able to help the other. I sought balance for myself and we have found balance for our relationship as well. I know I have much to learn. I have needed to feel in control all my life, influencing others whilst not allowing them to influence me. This is changing, but I have a lot to learn about how to let others in. I think it is the same for you. Together we are going to learn how to do this. Neither of us is perfect, but that is okay. We will have ups and downs, there will be difficulties at times which we will have to work through. We will both have fears and times of moving backwards into old ways of being. That is what relationships are all about, and through it all we will each be there for the other.'

'When did you get to be so wise?' he asked her.

The guide left them then: 'You don't need me now, but I will always hold you in my heart. There may be times in the future when I can be helpful again, but for now my work is done. Go forward and find the life that has always been waiting for you.'

She had set out on a journey to lose something, to lose the pain, the fear, the emptiness. She hadn't lost them, of course. They are part of being human. Instead she had found herself and all that she had buried. She was more real and alive now than she had ever been, and it felt good.

References

Bateman, A. W. & Fonagy, P. (2011) *Handbook of Mentalizing in Mental Health Practice*. Arlington, VA: American Psychiatric Publishing Inc.

Cozolino, L. (2016) *Why Therapy Works: Using Our Minds to Change Our Brains*. New York, NY: W. W. Norton & Co, Inc.

Fosha, D. (2000) *Transforming Power of Affect: A Model for Accelerated Change*. New York, NY: Basic Books.

Gilbert, P. (2009) *The Compassionate Mind*. London: Constable.

Golding, K. S. (2014) *Using Stories to Build Bridges with Traumatized Children: Creative Ideas for Therapy, Life Story Work, Direct Work and Parenting*. London: Jessica Kingsley Publishers.

Golding, K. S. & Gould, J. (2019) '"No Quick Fix": The Benefits of Longer Term Counselling for Birth Parents with Complex Histories of Trauma and Abuse: Carrie's Story,' in J. Alper (ed.) *Supporting Birth Parents Whose Children Have Been Adopted*, pp. 109–131. London: Jessica Kingsley Publishers.

Hodding Carter, W. (1953) *Where Main Street Meets the River*. New York, NY: Rinehart & Co.

Howe, D. (2005) *Child Abuse and Neglect: Attachment, Development and Intervention*. Hampshire: Palgrave Macmillan.

Hughes, D. A., Golding, K. S. & Hudson, J. (2019) *Healing Relational Trauma with Attachment-Focused Interventions: Dyadic Developmental Psychotherapy with Children and Families*. New York, NY: W. W. Norton & Co, Inc.

Karst, P. & Stevenson, G. (2001) *The Invisible String*. Camarillo, CA: De Vorss & Co.

Lee, D. with James, S. (2012) *The Compassionate Mind Approach for Recovering from Trauma Using Compassion Focused Therapy*. London: Robinson.

Nouwen, H. (2011) *Spiritual Formation: Following the Movements of the Spirit*. London: SPCK Publishing.

Perls, F. S. (1992) *Gestalt Therapy Verbatim*, 2nd edn. Gouldsboro, ME: Gestalt Journal Press.

Porges, S. W. (2017) *The Pocket Guide to the Polyvagal Theory: The Transformative Power of Feeling Safe*. New York, NY: W. W. Norton & Co, Inc.

Rogers, C. (1961) *On Becoming a Person: A Therapist's View of Psychotherapy*. London: Constable.

Trevarthen, C. (2001) 'Intrinsic motives for companionship in understanding: Their origin, development, and significance for infant mental health.' *Infant Mental Health Journal* 22, 95–131.

van der Kolk, B. (2014) *The Body Keeps the Score: Mind, Brain and Body in the Transformation of Trauma*. London: Penguin.

White, M. (2004) *Narrative Practice and Exotic Lives: Resurrecting Diversity in Everyday Life*. Adelaide, South Australia: Dulwich Centre Publications.

Index

Note: Page numbers of illustrations are given in *italics*